Color and Light in Man-made Environments

Color and Light in Man-made Environments

Frank H. Mahnke

Rudolf H. Mahnke

VNR Van Nostrand Reinhold Company

New York

Library of Congress Catalog Card Number 86-24656

ISBN 0-442-26080-6

Printed in the United States of America

Van Nostrand Reinhold Company Inc.
115 Fifth Avenue
New York, New York 10003

Van Nostrand Reinhold Company Limited
Molly Millars Lane
Wokingham, Berkshire RG11 2PY, England

Van Nostrand Reinhold
480 La Trobe Street
Melbourne, Victoria 3000, Australia

Macmillan of Canada
Division of Canada Publishing Corporation
164 Commander Boulevard
Agincourt, Ontario M1S 3C7, Canada

16 15 14 13 12 11 10 9 8 7 6 5 4 3 2

Library of Congress Cataloging-in-Publication Data

Mahnke, Frank H., 1947–
  Color and light in man-made environments.

  Bibliography: p.
  Includes index.
  1. Color—Psychological aspects. 2. Light—
Physiological effect. 3. Color in architecture.
4. Light in architecture. 5. Environmental psychology.
I. Mahnke, Rudolf H., 1925–   . II. Title.
BF789.C7M24 1987   729   86-24656
ISBN 0-442-26080-6

Contents

Preface

For many years, we have collected and kept abreast of research concerning the interaction between man and his environment—specifically, how he reacts to color and light on a psychological and a physiological basis. In order to apply environmental color effectively, man–environment relationships must be understood and an interdisciplinary approach must be adopted.

Our book is based upon this research. It has been written in a style that keeps the needs of the designer in mind, thereby making it a practical and useful guide.

We wish to express our gratitude and thanks to Faber Birren for his counsel in regard to the scope of this book, and for his help in the preparation of the material on visual display terminal offices.

Our thanks also go to Dr. Heinrich Frieling, Institute for Color Psychology (IFP), Marquartstein, West Germany; Dr. Philip C. Hughes, Director of Environmental Photobiology, Duro-Test Corporation, North Bergen, New Jersey; Dr. Rikard Küller, Docent, Environmental Psychology Unit, School of Architecture, Lund Institute of Technology, Lund, Sweden; Dr. John N. Ott, Director of the Environmental Health and Light Research Institute, Sarasota, Florida; and Dr. Thomas R.C. Sisson, Director of Neonatal Research, Professor of Pediatrics–UMDNJ, Newark Beth Israel Medical Center, Newark, New Jersey. All were of assistance in various ways.

Introduction

Color, or the concept of color, can be approached from different perspectives and different disciplines, such as the natural sciences, color theory, technology, philosophy, biology, medicine, psychology, and art. This book discusses color from the standpoint of designing the man-made environment, which to some extent involves all of these perspectives and disciplines.

Color is not the property of objects, spaces, or surfaces; it is the sensation caused by certain qualities of light that the eye recognizes and the brain interprets. Therefore, light and color are inseparable, and, in the design of the human habitat, equal attention must be devoted to their psychological, physiological, visual, aesthetical, and technical aspects.

This book presents relevant information for anyone in the business of creating artificial environments (such as the architect, interior designer/decorator, and color consultant). It is our aim to suggest that architects and designers need to adopt a new philosophy and perspective in their work with light and color. Architects, designers, city planners, and lighting engineers today are confronted more and more often with artificial environments and are faced with questions that they are ill-equipped to answer. The design community must adopt a new attitude toward scientific research conducted in many fields and covering many disciplines. The first consideration in the creation of interior and exterior man-made environments must be the evidence that has been accumulated concerning the interaction between man and his surroundings. Examining research material will aid designers in understanding the psychophysiological requirements for beneficial and healthy surroundings.

Color and light are major factors in man-made environments; their impact influences man's psychological reactions and physiological well-being. Research has proven that light and color affect the human organism on both a visual and a nonvisual basis. It is no longer valid to assume that the *only* significant role of light and color is to provide adequate illumination and a pleasant visual environment.

What is even more invalid, and incomprehensible as well, is the attitude of some skeptics who deny all of the scientific values, considering them sketchy or inconclusive. This mentality was developed decades ago, when research in color and light for the environment was considered to be in its infancy. An overwhelming amount of man–environment research has been conducted, but, for various reasons—one being a lack of interdisciplinary communication and investigation—the findings have not reached the design community with sufficient force to make a substantial impact.

In the 1981 annotated bibliography *Non-Visual Effects of Light and Colour*, a summary of the research related to physiological and psychological effects of light and color, the author and meticulous investigator Dr. Rikard Küller stated:

> During the course of this work it has become evident there is an enormous amount of facts and results that is almost never considered in practice and education. Thus, one finds a gap between research on one hand and practice on the other, the infamous application gap (Küller 1981, 238).

It has become evident to us in our work, which has been both investigative and practical, that an interdisciplinary approach to environmental design is the only solution in effectively dealing with and recognizing environmental problems. These problems also include potential psychological and physiological risks induced by environmental factors. Nervousness, headaches, lack of concentration, inefficiency, bad moods, visual problems, anxiety, and stress usually are blamed on everything except a guilty environment.

For all practical purposes, this book has two parts. The first part (chapters 1 through 8) discusses the importance of environmental conditions in regard to color and light and their effects on the human organism. In addition to being relevant to members of the design profession, this should also be of interest to developers, administrators, school officials, medical practitioners, and psychologists. In fact, we are *all* affected by our artificial surroundings. The second part (chapters 9 through 14) gives practical advice in the use of color and light for a variety of environments.

Besides answering the basic question of *"why"* and *"how,"* we believe it is useful to include a short review of color fundamentals, even though there is an abundant amount of published information available on such topics as color systems, color schemes, and contrast relationships. Since we are offering practical advice, we think that the inclusion of technical factors is more than warranted.

It is impossible to cover all aspects and data on color and light in one single work, but we have tried to make this book a fairly broad-based reference work for anyone interested or professionally involved in man-made environments. We hope it will be a useful tool, but we hope most of all that it will inspire further interest and investigation into man–environment relationships.

Psychophysiological Effects

Color, which is created by light, is therefore a form of energy, and this energy affects body function just as it influences mind and emotion. Today, thanks to sophisticated techniques of research and analysis, we know that color affects cortical activation (brain waves), functions of the autonomic nervous system (which regulates the body's internal environment), and hormonal activity, and that color arouses definite emotional and aesthetic associations. In short, our response to color is total; it influences us both psychologically and physiologically.

A NEUROPSYCHOLOGICAL ASPECT

Although knowledge about brain functions is still dim, scientists do recognize that there is an intimate relationship between this complex organ and human behavior. Stimulating the brain can make people feel angry, happy, or sexy. It also causes the movement of specific muscles, evokes various behavior patterns, and can create complex hallucinations. It is virtually common knowledge that damage to the brain may produce such results as disturbances of speech, hearing, or sight; disruption of muscle control; and coma.

Neuropsychologists study these relationships by examining the

1

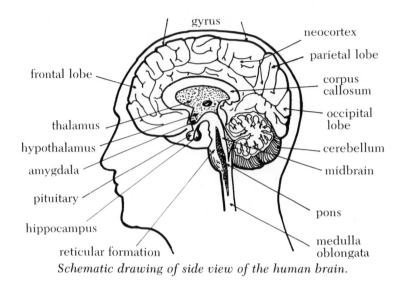

Schematic drawing of side view of the human brain.

structure of the nervous system and how it relates to organs and other parts of the body. They also seek to discover how information coming from the environment (exterior) and from within is changed into feelings, thoughts, and actions. An understanding of the relationship between the brain and the action of muscles and glands also falls within the realm of the neuropsychologist.

In 1949, G. Moruzzi and H.W. Magoun published observations that proved important in understanding our general reactions to stimulation. The central nervous system (CNS), consisting of the brain and spinal cord, is the major control center for all human behavior. The investigators found that every impulse transmitted by afferent nerves that reaches the higher centers of the CNS first activates part of the brain stem, the reticular formation, which then activates the entire nervous system. The reticular formation seems to affect the entire nervous system's state of preparedness. This has been designated the *ascending reticular activation system* (ARAS).

Man is subjected to many kinds of stimulation, including information from the visual field, and all of it affects the ARAS. As Küller has explained (1981), "The ARAS might be regarded as a clearing station for all kinds of stimulation ranging from sensory deprivation at one extreme to sensory overload at the other." Much of the information from the visual field (or visual stimulation) lies in the hands of the designer, who therefore must understand basics of the activation theory. This will become especially evident in regard to environmental over- and understimulation, discussed later in this chapter.

Moruzzi and Magoun's theory has been revised in various ways. Reticular activation occurs not only through external stimulation but also through mental activity—impulses coming from the highest nervous centers. The cognitive mechanism—perception, memory, and judgment—is then triggered to deal with a great part of the incoming information. These impulses descend from the cortex on the reticular formation. Therefore, there are two functional systems; in addition to the ascending reticular activation system, there is the *descending reticular activation system* (DRAS). Man's arousal level may be influenced via the ARAS, before the impulse has reached the cortex, or via the DRAS, after the cortex has had the time to make an analysis.

Activation is divided into two components called *phasic arousal* and *tonic arousal*. Phasic arousal implies the immediate response to stimulation, while tonic arousal is the response level averaged over a prolonged period. The tonic arousal level changes gradually either upward or downward, depending on the occurrence of phasic arousal reactions. The participating reticular formation seeks to maintain a state of normalcy in the arousal level during this process, but it can also malfunction, as has been shown in experiments on sensory deprivation and in stress research. (*See* Unity and Complexity Balance—Variety Within Reason, later in this chapter.)

In sum, every impulse, whether originated externally or internally, results in a short temporary arousal reaction (phasic). Repeated effect will alter the tonic arousal level either upward or downward. At that point, there are changes in the individual's emotional state.

RED VERSUS BLUE AND GREEN

Since the 1949 study by Moruzzi and Magoun, there have been numerous investigations of the effects of visual stimulation upon the ARAS. Perhaps the studies best known in the design world are those that compare the light of long wavelengths to that of short wavelengths, or red versus blue or green surroundings.

As early as 1942, K. Goldstein published his observations on the influence of color on the functioning of the organism. In this work he also pointed out some normal effects on motor behavior. Perhaps his most classic study was that of patients suffering from Parkinson's disease. It showed that red colors had a tendency to worsen a patient's pathological condition, whereas green colors seemed to improve it. Goldstein also found, among many observations, that brain-damaged subjects responded excitedly to red and calmly to green. Although Goldstein's theories have been attacked because his subjects were brain-damaged, his overall findings have withstood the challenges.

R. Gerard found in 1957 that red had a more arousing effect than did blue on visual cortical activity and functions of the autonomic nervous system. M.R. Ali in 1972, using EEG (electroencephalogram) analysis, demonstrated greater arousal following red light than blue light. K.W. Jacobs and F.E. Hustmyer (1974) noted that red was more arousing than green, and green more arousing than blue or yellow. Together, these studies seem to indicate that colors richer in longer wavelengths are more arousing than those of short wavelengths.

Partly because of these findings, it is often concluded erroneously that exposure to a red room, for example, will have a continuously higher arousal effect. In fact, exposure to any single strong hue will cause an immediate reaction that can be measured easily, but the duration of the effect is not continuous. Red, again as an example, may stimulate, but after a length of time, bodily responses may fall below normal. If a red room, unrelieved by other hues, is considered aggravating, then that is because of its limited visual stimulation, not because of a temporary higher arousal effect. The greater concern in regard to psychophysiological effects or response revolves around variety—the lack or overuse of it.

UNITY AND COMPLEXITY BALANCE—VARIETY WITHIN REASON

If we measure balance by the visual information rate contained in a space, such as a room, as it is perceived through the optical system, we can identify two opposite poles called *unity* and *complexity*. Unity involves various components and parts fitting together into a coherent unit. Complexity involves more variation.

Extreme unity (monotony or sensory deprivation) can lead to understimulation and extreme complexity to overstimulation. Exposure to overstimulation can cause changes in the rate of breathing, pulse rate, and blood pressure; increase in muscle tension; psychiatric reactions of varying types; and probably compounded medical consequences, such as increased susceptibility to infection, coronary disease, and ulcers. The "stress research" conducted in the 1960s and 1970s showed that these symptoms are typical effects on those persons who have been subjected to overstimulation.

Persons subjected to understimulation showed symptoms of restlessness, excessive emotional response, difficulty in concentration, irritation, and, in some cases, a variety of more extreme reactions. This conclusion should be taken to heart by those who propose a white or neutral environment; such environments are anything but neutral in the effects they have on the occupants.

Rikard Küller's paper entitled "The Use of Space—Some Physiological and Philosophical Aspects" described an experiment on the effects of two opposite environments. He summarized the experiment this way:

> The research subjects, six men and six women, were placed in two rooms in balanced order for a period of three hours. The one room was grey and sterile, the other colourful and diversified. The two rooms differed in visual complexity and visual unity but not in pleasantness. Measurements taken during the first, second and third hour showed that the subjects generally experienced a lack of emotional control in the colourful room. The chaotic visual impact made them feel silent and subdued. Also, the alpha-component [alpha brain-wave activity] of the EEG was considerably lower in the colourful room than in the grey one as long as the subjects' eyes were open. This difference disappeared more or less when the subjects closed their eyes. The difference in alpha level between the subjects in the two rooms can be explained in terms of cortical arousal. Stress reactions were more noticeable in men than in women. The men also become more bored in the grey room. In contrast to the women they might not have been able to relax mentally although there was little to look at. This assumption is supported by a general clinical experience, namely that stress and tension diseases occur more often and more seriously in men than in women. Subjects' EKG (heart rate) was slower in the colourful room than in the grey one, which is in agreement with a hypothesis of Lacey, Kagan, Lacey and Moss, 1963, i.e., intense attention might be accompanied by cardiac deceleration. Thus, it was demonstrated that colouring and visual patterning of the interior space might have a profound physiological and psychological effect and this effect might vary between different groups of subjects (Küller 1981, 101).

Thus, Küller demonstrated that color (or its absence) and pattern in the visual environment have a profound effect on the EEG and the pulse rate, as well as on the subjective emotional feelings experienced by the subjects. This corroborates the fact that the ARAS affects not only the cortex but the entire autonomic nervous system.

It is especially interesting to note that brain-wave activity was lower in the colorful room than in the gray room and heart response was slower in the colorful room. Therefore, we may conclude that a dull environment tends to prod brain activity, which may induce anxiety, fear, and distress.

Just as light and color affect the ARAS, so does visual pattern. A number of studies have been conducted—making use of such factors as size, color, contrast, shape, and brightness—to investigate the arousal effect of pattern. Berlyne and McDonnell (1965), for example, found that more complex or incongruous visual patterns evoke an increase in phasic arousal level.

In some interior design work there is a marked tendency toward the use of multicolored stripes on walls, cutout designs integrated into carpeting, gaudy floral or geometric wallcoverings, and bright hues. The previously discussed problems of the overstimulating environment will manifest themselves as a result of this practice. Overexcitation *is* distracting and fatiguing. Strong color, too much visual pattern, and high brightness demand voluntary and involuntary attention. Vivid design in work areas can impair productivity by seriously interfering with work tasks that require visual concentration.

On the other hand, we know now that the understimulated environment is as unacceptable as the overstimulated one. Taking all research collectively, it is safe to conclude and suggest that color variety is psychologically most beneficial. It is not just that one color is better than another for a specific purpose, that one may be considered psychologically exciting or another calming, but a variety of visual stimulation and change in atmosphere is required in establishing a sound milieu. M.D. Vernon, a British psychologist, has written:

Thus we must conclude that normal consciousness, perception and thought can be maintained only in a constantly changing environment. When there is no change, a state of "sensory deprivation" occurs; the capacity of adults to concentrate deteriorates, attention fluctuates and lapses, and normal perception fades (Vernon, quoted in Birren 1982, 28).

In the total environment there must be colors in changing degrees of brightness, temperature (warm and cool colors), and chromatics (strong and weak), and the complementary of the dominant color should be present to some extent. Maximum favorable color effects depend on variety and contrast, within reason.

The need for variety has been summed up best by Faber Birren:

> In response to environment, people expect all of their senses to be moderately stimulated at all times. This is what happens in nature, and it relates not only to color and changing degrees of brightness, but to variations in temperature and sound. The unnatural condition is one that is static, boring, tedious and unchanging. Variety is indeed the spice—and needed substance—of life (Birren 1983, 167).

The principle of unity and complexity balance is perhaps one of the major difficulties that the designer may encounter, and at the same time it is one of great importance. The concept is not new. Writers on the subject of color have expressed similar views over the years. It matters little whether their conclusions were based on research of the day or keen observation, since present-day scientific investigations validate their pronouncements. As Frederick M. Crewdson wrote:

> Balance is the securing of unity in the midst of variety. Both variety and unity are necessary to sustain interest, and these opposing forces must be balanced. Variety is necessary to attract and arouse interest; unity is essential to create a favorable impression and to satisfy the moods and desires. Variety overdone is confusing and unpleasant; unity overdone is monotonous. The mark of good color arrangement is in knowing where to stop between these two extremes (Crewdson 1953, 121).

In 1963, Richard Ellinger had this to say about complexity:

> First of all, as human beings exposed to the visual stimuli, we are, let us admit, easily confused. Disorder occasioned by unrestrained diversity can be nothing but emotionally repellent. We have a limited tolerance for diversity (Ellinger 1963, 27).

In regard to unity, the same author commented:

A second human demand is rooted in our emotional response to tedium. We are easily bored. We can easily get too much of anything. Emotionally, we demand relief whenever monotony threatens. We demand the play of opposing forces (Ellinger 1963, 27).

Judging where "balance" is achieved depends on the degree to which the designer has developed his color faculties and sensitivity. This demands knowledge of relationships among harmony, contrast, and the affective values of color. These factors will be discussed thoroughly in the chapters that follow.

PERSONALITY AND REACTION TO STIMULATION

Another important consideration in creating beneficial environments is individuals' reaction tendencies—how their personalities affect their reactions to stimulation. All people have pleasant or unpleasant arousal reactions, but they experience them in varying degrees. The psychologist H.J. Eysenck designated these reactions as *extroversion* and *introversion*, terms that express the degree of excitability.

There is a fallacious tradition among designers to prescribe passive environments for the extroverted temperaments in order to calm them down, and active environments for the subdued and introverted personalities to draw them out of their introspection and boost their spirits. Quite the opposite will occur; neither will be happier in surroundings contrary to his personality. The nervous system of the introvert is more excitable than that of the extrovert. The afferent flow of stimulation, regardless of its origin, is facilitated in the introvert but obstructed in the extrovert. In other words, there is a difference in the amount of stimulation passing through the cerebral cortex for each of these personality types.

In general terms, this means that the extroverted personality type has a greater inclination toward more intensive stimulation, and consequently enjoys more colorful surroundings with warmer hues. In fact, incorrect environmental conditions for the extroverted personality can lead to a lack of interest, boredom, and an exploratory mode of behavior that in extreme cases can become a stimulus craving with pathological side effects. On the other hand, because introverts are very sensitive to stimulation and have a great need for privacy and calm, they manage best in environments with cool hues and a lower degree of stimulation. For them, overstimulated environments will lead to intensive anxiety or psychosomatic symptoms.

Although for normal people it is better that their surroundings match instead of contrast with their personalities, it has been written (Birren 1967) that for people with some forms of mental illness this method might have to be reversed. Color has been used therapeutically in treating emotionally and mentally ill patients, in the belief that manic and aggressive patients need cool colors to calm them down, while depressive and suicidal patients need warm and exciting colors to compensate for the melancholic inner state.

A patient in a frantic or manic state may be sedated by the use of cool hues and dim illumination, just as a depressive patient may have his spirits bolstered by compensating warm and stimulating hues, which will direct his attention toward the environment and away from his inner state. These, then, are immediate therapeutic effects of temporary duration. This visual sedation or stimulation, whichever the case may be, cannot be prolonged, because it will lose its effectiveness in a relatively short time. Also, the concept of unity and complexity balance indicates that color reactions, to be beneficial and actively maintained, require constant change.

It should not be difficult to set aside certain areas where color can have an immediate therapeutic effect. Most mental facilities already have rooms set aside for distraught patients. These "quiet rooms" should be color-treated to achieve the desired therapeutic effect. Colors in patient rooms can also be alternated—cooler hues for one and warmer hues for another—to provide some assistance with the introvert/extrovert reaction tendencies.

Characteristics and Effects of Major Hues

Color not only produces mood associations, subjective and objective impressions, but also influences our estimation of volume, weight, time, temperature, and noise. Collective findings have shown that there are basic reactions to color common to most people.

Numerous studies have been undertaken that show the affective values of certain hues, thereby making it possible to assess mood-tones of colors with reasonable accuracy. One such study, conducted by K. Warner Schaie (1961), analyzed the associations among eleven adjectival mood descriptions as well as the term *pleasant* with ten colors. Values in his scale showed reasonably good replication from one group of raters to the other. Some colors were found to be associated with several mood-tones and some mood-tones were associated with more than one color.

It has often been questioned whether cultural heritage influences the effects of color, thus rendering meaningless any reasonable conclusions about color's psychological effects. Each culture has its own color and pattern traditions, and of course there are economic, geographical, and religious factors, as well as fluctuations of taste and educational levels.

Studies on color connotations performed in Sweden and

Greece showed that the Greeks considered all colors to be equally refined while the Swedes considered saturated colors to be more vulgar than unsaturated ones (Sivik 1969). Purple, the traditional color of mourning among many peoples, is disapproved of in six Asian countries. Other examples are numerous, since a fair amount of research has been done on the subject. Yet, taking all the research collectively, we can state safely that there are universal elements in color where broad appeal as a practical necessity is an attainable goal. In the physiological realm, there are those some of color and pattern that are outside the scope of how the individual might feel about them. Perhaps the answer to the whole question has been summarized best by Küller:

> One of the most striking features of the results concerning preferences, connotations and color-mood associations is the consistency from one individual to another, from group to group and cross-culturally. There has been a great number of cross-cultural studies comparing subjects in America, Lebanon, Kenya, Botswana, Greece, just to mention a few. Monkeys have been compared to Man, men to women, children to adults, laymen to architects. As one author concludes: "It would indicate either that our heritage is such that we learn the correct responses, or that there is some innate mood reaction to different colors" (Küller 1981).

Below, for convenient reference, is an overview of the general effects and efficacy of major hues.

HUE EFFECT—IMPRESSIONS OR ASSOCIATIONS— CHARACTER

Red

- *Hue effect*: exciting (bright red); stimulating (red)
- *Impressions or associations*: positive—passionate, fervid, active, strong, warm; negative—aggressive, raging, intense, fierce, bloody
- *Character*: Red is perhaps the most dominant and dynamic of all colors. It grabs the attention and overrules all other hues. The lens of the eye has to adjust to focus the red light wavelengths; their natural focal point lies behind the retina. Thus, red advances, creating the illusion that red objects are closer than they are.

Symbolically, red means fire, life, and strength, but its aggressive masculine nature is also linked with combat, dominance, war, and rebellion. The dynamic nature changes dramatically where the color turns pink. It changes its gender to feminine and appears gentle and acquiescent.

Orange

- *Hue effect*: exciting (bright orange); stimulating (orange); cheering (light orange)
- *Impressions or associations*: positive—jovial, lively, energetic, extroverted, sociable; negative—intrusive, blustering (if color is highly saturated)
- *Character*: Orange is mellower and less primitive than red. It has virtually no negative cultural or emotional associations. Aesthetically, though, desaturated hues may appear cheap and without vigor.

Yellow

- *Hue effect*: cheering
- *Impressions or associations*: positive—sunny, cheerful, radiant, vital, high-spirited; negative—egocentric, glaring
- *Character*: In pure form, yellow is the happiest of all colors. It radiates warmth, cheerfulness, and inspiration. Yellow is a comparatively light color; as it loses its lightness, when modified, it ceases to be yellow. Symbolically, yellow signifies enlightenment (mental and spiritual), expansion, sunlight, and communication.

Green

- *Hue effect*: retiring (light green); relaxing (green)
- *Impressions or associations*: positive—tranquil, refreshing, quiet, natural; negative—common, tiresome, guilty
- *Character*: Psychologically, green represents a withdrawal from stimulus. Since the lens of the eye focuses green light exactly on the retina, it is also the most restful color to the eye.

Color has a character, as do humans, that often has two or more sides. In the case of green, these are full of contradictions. In its symbolic value or image, this hue represents the power of nature, of life. Yet it is also the color of mold, decay, and sickness in humans.

Blue

- *Hue effect*: retiring (light blue); relaxing (blue)
- *Impressions or associations*: positive—calm, secure, comfortable, sober, contemplative; negative—frightening, depressing, melancholy, cold
- *Character*: In all aspects, blue is the antithesis of red. In its appearance, blue is transparent and wet; red is opaque and dry. Psychologically, the cool and relaxing nature of blue is in direct opposition to the warmth and excitement of red. While red seems vulgar at times, blue exhibits a noble character. In its action upon the human organism, blue will decrease blood pressure and pulse rate while red will have the opposite effect (followed by a reversal in both cases after a period of time).

Purple

- *Hue effect*: subduing
- *Impressions or associations*: positive—dignified, exclusive; negative—lonely, mournful, pompous, conceited
- *Character*: Purple is a blend of red and blue, the two colors that are physically and psychologically most opposed. In its various tones, purple may evoke delicacy and richness or appear unsettling and degenerate. Violet is a lighter shade of purple and a pure spectral hue. Purple is a mixed color. The two encompass vast differentations in hue.

COLOR EFFECTS IN THE INTERIOR SPACE

The location (top, sides, bottom) of a color stimulus within the interior space can make a great deal of difference in influencing a room's character, the way it is perceived psychologically, and the subsequent reactions to it. A particular hue that is perfectly suitable on the floor may elicit an entirely different reaction when applied to the ceiling.

Red

- Ceiling: intruding, disturbing, heavy
- Walls: aggressive, advancing
- Floor: conscious, alert

In practical situations, pure red is seldom used, except as an accent. Although physiological arousal may be temporary, red psychologically exhibits the characteristics shown above. The overuse of saturated red adds to the complexity within a space. Modifications of pure red are much more suitable.

Pink

- Ceiling: delicate, comforting, or too intimate, depending on individual inclination
- Walls: aggression-inhibiting, weak, too sweet if not grayed
- Floor: perhaps too delicate, unfamiliar in this location

Brown

- Ceiling: oppressive and heavy (if dark)
- Walls: secure and assuring if wood, much less so if paint
- Floor: steady, stable

The designer must be careful in using brown in certain institutions, as it may evoke fecal associations.

Orange

- Ceiling: stimulating, attention-seeking
- Walls: warm, luminous
- Floor: activating, motion-oriented

This hue is more mellow than red and has more livable charm. Reflection on the skin may enhance some skin tones.

Yellow

- Ceiling: light (if toward lemon), luminous, stimulating
- Walls: warm (if toward orange), exciting to irritating (if highly saturated)
- Floor: elevating, diverting

Because of its high visibility, yellow serves many safety purposes, especially in industrial environments. It also appears brighter than white and is useful in poorly illuminated and dim spaces.

Green

- Ceiling: protective (reflection on skin can be unattractive)
- Walls: cool, secure, calm, reliable, passive, irritating if glaring (electric green)
- Floor: natural (up to a certain saturation point), soft, relaxing, cold (if toward blue-green)

Green, along with blue-green, provides a good environment for meditation and tasks involving high concentration.

Blue

- Ceiling: celestial, cool, less tangibly advancing (if light), heavy and oppressive (if dark)
- Walls: cool and distant (if light), encouraging and space-deepening (if dark)
- Floor: inspiring feeling of effortless movement (if light), substantial (if dark)

Blue tends to be cold and bleak if applied to large areas, especially in hallways and long corridors. Medium or deep tones are appropriate in incidental areas. Pale blue is refracted sharply by the lens of the eye and therefore tends to cast a haze over details and objects in the environment. This may cause distress to some people confined to a particular area for a long period.

Purple

Seldom used in the interior space except for incidental areas. In large spaces it may disturb the focus of the eye. Psychologically, it may appear disconcerting and subduing.

Gray

- Ceiling: shadowy
- Walls: neutral to boring
- Floor: neutral

As is the case with all neutral hues, gray fails to have much psychotherapeutic application. A recent design trend is to use it in conjunction with pink, purple, or purple-red tones in accent walls and furnishings. The practice has permeated all types of environments, from restaurants to health facilities. This defies all logic and is in direct opposition to many of the principles presented in this book.

White
- Ceiling: empty (no design objections—helps to diffuse light sources and reduce shadows)
- Walls: neutral, empty, sterile, without energy
- Floor: touch-inhibiting (not to be walked upon)

There are psychological and physiological justifications for not using white or off-white as a dominant color in the majority of environments. For details, see chapter 3.

Black
- Ceiling: hollow to oppressive
- Walls: ominous, dungeonlike
- Floor: odd, abstract

CENTRIFUGAL/CENTRIPETAL ACTION AND COMPLEXITY

In meeting design objectives, it must be stressed that the mood or atmosphere of a space can be manipulated to conform with the function of that space. The degree of mood creation depends on the particular color usage. Warm and luminous colors with high levels of light produce a centrifugal action, directing attention outward and toward the environment. Such environments are conducive to cheerfulness, action, and muscular effort. A general office space, where no one performs tasks that demand high concentration, should not have the same surroundings as a recreational area, although both spaces may want to appear cheerful, warm, and friendly.

Softer surroundings, cooler colors, and lower levels of illumination produce a centripetal action. Such an environment furthers inward orientation and enhances the ability to concentrate. This fact can be put to good use in areas where employees are required to perform difficult visual and mental tasks.

As to color and complexity, there is a high correlation between the strength (chromaticity) of a color and the perceived excitement of a space. Studies in full-scale rooms indicate that complexity increases as chromatic strength increases. Strong colors will make a room appear exciting; weak colors give an impression of calmness, regardless of hue. Color contrast also contributes to the apparent excitement of a space.

PERCEPTION OF VOLUME

Lightness is one of the most important factors in the perception of openness in the interior space. Light or pale colors recede and increase the apparent room size, as do cooler colors and small patterns.

Dark or saturated hues protrude and decrease the apparent size of a room. In general, it may also be said that warm colors and large patterns have the same effect.

A high illumination level will enlarge the appearance of volume, whereas a low illumination level will diminish it. A point to consider—which may not have a direct relationship to volume—is that of light entering through a window. The wall opposite a window generally should be kept fairly light, or it will absorb much of the daylight and cause uneven illumination. Window wall, window frame, and sill should also be light; otherwise, the contrast between wall and the natural light will cause irritating glare.

PERCEPTION OF WEIGHT AND SIZE

In general, darker colors appear heavier, whereas lighter and less saturated (pastel) ones seem less dense. If the hues are of the same value and intensity, the tendency is to perceive the warmer hues as heavier.

Good use of these effects can be made in factories and workshops. Bases for machinery and equipment will appear steadier and more solid if they are painted darker than the equipment itself. A piece of heavy machinery painted dark green, for example, will seem imbalanced, shaky, and awkward if it rests on yellow feet.

Heavy objects designed to be moved, carried, or thrown by human effort may be made to appear less heavy with lighter and cooler colors. Cool colors will also make things appear shorter and smaller; warm colors make them seem longer and larger. It is essential to make such color design decisions on location and with consideration of the whole.

In regard to general interiors, extremely high ceilings may be painted in darker and warmer hues. The heaviness of the darker hue, with its characteristic of advancing, will make the ceiling appear lower. Likewise, low ceilings will appear higher if painted in light, cool tones.

ESTIMATION OF TIME

There seems to be a contradiction in regard to the effect of color on the perception of time. It is generally believed that in environments with warm colors, time is overestimated. With cool colors, on the other hand, the opposite appears to be true: Time is underestimated.

An experiment (Goldstein, in Clark 1975) that seems to substantiate this belief was conducted with two groups of salesmen. Having removed their watches, one group attended a meeting in a red room, the other in a green one. The "red" group guessed that it had spent twice as much time in the meeting, whereas the "green" group thought it had spent less time in the meeting than it actually had.

In addition, Goldstein noted that under the influence of red light, time is overestimated. Under green and blue light, the judgment of time is in the opposite direction. However, a study conducted by an American psychologist produced opposite results (Porter and Mikellides 1976). Two identical twenty-minute lectures were presented to two separate audiences; one was seated in a blue lecture theater and the other in a red one. The audience in the blue theater felt rather bored and was under the impression that the lecture had lasted longer than it did. The group in the red theater found that time had passed quickly and the lecture had been interesting.

Findings of an experiment performed by a British university were similar. Participants in a meeting held in brightly colored surroundings judged it to have lasted forty-five minutes less than another held in a subtly colored room.

Although there is as yet no resolution to the question of which hues affect the over- or underestimation of time, it can be concluded from these experiments that color apparently influences the judgment of time.

PERCEPTION OF TEMPERATURE

A long-favored hypothesis maintains that color has the power to suggest warmth or coolness. People are fairly unanimous in their opinions of the colors that visually induce either effect.

In his book *The Elements of Color*, Johannes Itten tells of experiments that demonstrated a difference of five to seven degrees in the subjective feeling of heat or cold between a workroom painted blue-green and one painted red-orange. Occupants of the blue-green room felt that 59°F was cold, whereas the temperature had to fall to 52° to 54°F in the red-orange room before the subjects felt cold.

Another example (Clark 1975) is that of an air-conditioned factory cafeteria with light-blue walls. Employees complained of the cold, although the temperature was set at 72°F. Nor did the complaints stop when the thermostat was raised to 75°F. The walls were repainted orange and the 75°F temperature setting, then considered too warm, was reduced to 72°F.

A Norwegian study produced similar results. People tended to set the thermostat four degrees higher in a blue room than in a red room (Porter and Mikellides 1976).

Colors also absorb and retain heat in various degrees, depending on their light-reflection ratio. The lighter the color, the more light (therefore heat) is reflected; the darker the color, the more light is absorbed. In the practical application of color, however, it is important to consider the visual inducement of temperature sensation over the absorption factor. Cool colors should be applied in locations where people are exposed to high temperatures, and vice versa.

PERCEPTION OF NOISE AND SOUND

Phenomena in which sounds will affect color perception have been reviewed by Gestalt psychologists such as Heinz Werner. Kravkov, Allen, and Schwartz (quoted in Birren 1982) found that loud noises and strong odors and tastes make the eye more sensitive to green and less sensitive to red.

For design purposes, the designer may profit from the relationship between noise and color that is more of a poetic nature or mental association. Stimulation of the senses, brightness, and loudness are associated with the most active effect of warm colors, the reverse being true for cool colors. People mentally connect a loud red with one of high saturation. Rarely does anyone speak of a loud blue or green. High-pitched and shrill sounds tend to be compared with saturated and light hues.

These associations can be used to compensate visually for noise problems, especially in work environments such as industrial plants. A noisy environment will be experienced subjectively as noisier or more bothersome if painted with glaring yellows or reds. Shrill and high-pitched sounds may be offset by olive green. Muffled sounds appear more so in darker-hued surroundings, and lighter colors, such as light, clean greens (slightly toward yellow), can be used to compensate.

ASSOCIATIONS OF ODOR AND TASTE

Colors that hold pleasant associations with smell are pink, lavender, pale yellow, and green. Tints of coral, peach, soft yellow, light green, turquoise, flamingo, and pumpkin have pleasant associations with taste.

Some industries (such as food processing or perfume making) produce odors that, whether agreeable or not, may be so penetrating as to become a nuisance. It is almost possible to "taste" the smell. The association of certain colors with particular odors only exacerbates the problem. A solution is to use colors that are contrary in their association to the problem odor. (For details, see chapter 14.)

A POINT TO REMEMBER

The preceding analysis of the general effects of color stimulus, mostly based on psychological studies, should be helpful in evaluating a particular environment and conducive to improving the function, performance of tasks, and elimination of or decrease in problems of volume, temperature, and noise within individual spaces.

It must be reemphasized strongly that the environment in its entirety—whether it be a hospital, school, or industrial plant—must have a variety of color. The psychological power of one color will never satisfy all of the needs of an environment. It would be a great error to conclude that the psychological reaction to a particular hue—even if it varies somewhat in hue position, chroma, and value—is sufficient justification to use it in all the spaces within an environment. A psychiatric hospital will not be "relaxing" all in greens just because that is an inherent characteristic of that color. The principle of unity and complexity balance must be satisfied at all times, and various color effects are an aid in achieving that balance.

THREE

The Case Against White

For years, the use of white and off-white in interiors was so common that it reached epidemic proportions. The advent of white walls began around 1955 and reached its peak in 1975. More recently, there have been claims that this practice is diminishing. Perhaps it is, but at a very slow pace—slow enough to warrant another call for an immediate halt to white and off-white interiors.

We have visited several newly built environments, medical facilities in particular, where the predominant color of the interior was still off-white. One was a facility housing children suffering from cancer. Especially here, it should have been realized that white walls would hardly lessen the patients' mental anguish. Color could have been used effectively to create a cheerful surrounding, thereby drawing attention outward and away from inner distress.

Some designers now are employing white as part of a "neutral color" design trend, along with gray. This is especially evident in new office buildings. The supposed purpose of this is to reflect our modern technological world in terms of unadorned, clean, efficient, impersonal, futuristic surroundings—technology, space travel, and computers translated into interior design. The idea that business efficiency must be reflected by surroundings devoid of color defies logical explanation. This trend is on the rise, and it might not be too incorrect to speculate that white may have a resurgence.

During our many years of collecting reference material on color and light, we have not yet come across any pronouncement that supports the use of white and off-white on psychological or physiological grounds. As early as 1947, Louis Cheskin wrote: "White walls, as we know, are an optical strain and a psychological hazard." Over the years, this simple truth has been echoed again and again by many who have been concerned with color beyond its decorative value. In 1984, a West German agency issued a study by Heinrich Frieling on color in the work environment. Its conclusion about white walls: neutral, empty, without vitality.

On a psychological basis, white is sterile. Unless negation is the desired result, it fails to have much psychotherapeutic value. In psychological color-preference tests, this bleak and emotionless hue is at the bottom of the list. It has been noted that reaction to white is one of bored disinterest. K. Warner Schaie, employing a color pyramid test, found that the incidence of the use of white and black was significantly higher among schizophrenics than among normal persons (quoted in Birren 1978). Hardly anyone will choose white over "color."

It is often argued by designers that white in interiors is an ideal background for the introduction of colored decorative effects. Regardless of the introduction of color in decorative items, the main characteristic or impression of the environment more than likely will remain white. Also, the contrast between white and highly colored decorative effects may require extreme adaptive changes from light to dark—a cause of eye fatigue. On the other hand, colors of low saturation set against white will look bland and commonplace.

Those who found the "hospital green" of the past unpleasant because of its institutional associations can place white in the same category. Psychologists now are in general agreement that institutions should look anything but institutional; white runs contrary to that school of thought. Its use has tragic effects in old-age or convalescent homes, where many are confined indoors for the greater part of the day. People need sensory variety, and this includes color. Monotony only induces anxiety, tension, fear, and distress. Environments that are predominantly neutral in appearance (white, gray) are beyond any positive value and will always appear static, boring, and tedious. It is also doubtful that a hospitalized person, perhaps already near the mental breaking point, under emotional strain, or recovering from surgical treatment, will have his spirits lifted by a preponderance of white walls.

White, when accompanied by high levels of natural or artificial light, may also play havoc with human vision. High environmental brightness demands fatiguing action of the eye muscles by severely constricting the pupil opening. It handicaps vision by producing distressing glare akin to snow blindness. Prolonged exposure to high brightness can cause damage to the visual organ, or further aggravate existing eye problems.

To illustrate the point, we quote Armando Valladares, a former political prisoner in Cuba, from the August 15, 1983, issue of *Time* magazine:

> By August, the authorities had built special premises so as to keep me in utter solitary confinement. The walls and ceiling were painted dazzling white, and just above my head, my jailers installed ten neon tubes about five feet long. These were kept on all the time, throwing off a blinding light that caused my sight to be damaged.

Many complaints of eyestrain often can be corrected by removing the glare of walls without changing the light levels. Had architects and designers adhered to recommended light-reflection levels, the use of white and off-white might never have come about. Recommended reflectances for wall surfaces have always been 40 to 60 percent, which can be stretched, depending on the overall lighting situation, to about 70 percent. The minimum light reflectance level of off-white, warm, or cool tones is approximately 81 percent and increases at times to over 94 percent. Most paint manufacturers list the light-reflection value of each color on their color samples, thereby eliminating any guesswork.

White need not be used as a predominant color; there are too many better alternatives. Often it is used as a matter of expediency, or by those not yet sure of themselves in their approaches to color. In this respect, white is considered a "safe" color, evoking neither a positive nor a negative comment. People have been conditioned to white by its overabundant use. None of these reasons justify aesthetically and psychologically sterile environments that may also create a hazard to vision.

Color Fundamentals

This chapter provides a brief review of the color fundamentals that a designer must know in his everyday work. It is brief because entire books have been written on this topic alone. (A list of recommended references appears in the Bibliography. Some of these may be out of print, but copies are available in major libraries.)

The color examples that follow are based on the Munsell ten-hue color wheel. (More about the Munsell system of color appears later in the chapter.) Among beginning students of color, confusion often arises because some writers differ in their color notations in their explanations of color systems. For example, in some references the complement of red is identified as green, and in others as blue-green. This is not a matter of differences in color, but of differences in the divisions of various color wheels, and color identification. The twelve-hue color wheel, for example, is divided into red, red-orange, orange, yellow-orange, yellow, yellow-green, green, blue-green, blue, blue-violet, violet, and red-violet, while the Munsell ten-hue color-wheel divisions are red, yellow-red, yellow, green-yellow, green, blue-green, blue, purple-blue, purple, and red-purple.

THE COLOR ATTRIBUTES: HUE, SATURATION, AND LIGHTNESS

Hue is the quality or characteristic by which one color is distinguished from another. The elementary hues that we differentiate are based on the spectral hues red, orange, yellow, green, blue, and violet. All colors are judged to be similar to one hue or a proportion of two of the spectral hues. Thus crimson, vermilion, and pink are close in hue, although they are different colors. Physically, hue is determined by wavelength.

White, gray, and black are perceived as colorless, being neither reddish, yellowish, greenish, or bluish. This lack of color (chroma) causes them to be termed achromatic.

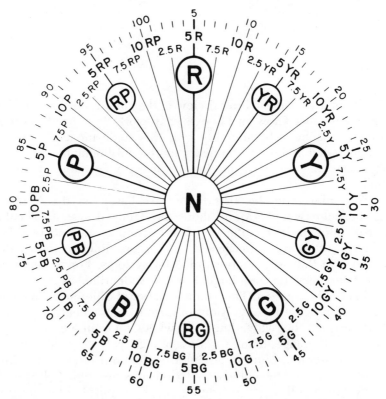

Hue symbols and their relationship to one another (courtesy of Munsell Color).

Saturation is the second attribute by which a color is distinguished. Also referred to as strength, intensity, or chroma, it designates the purity of a given color, the quality that distinguishes it from a grayed color. Two colors may be the same in hue (for instance, two greens), and one no lighter or darker than the other, yet still appear different in color strength.

Lightness, or its synonymic *value*, is the third dimension in the description of color. It is the quality that differentiates a dark color from a light one. The lightness of a pigment is a measure of how much light is reflected from its surface. Sometimes brightness is used as a synonym for lightness—which may be confusing. Brightness means the intensity of a light source or a luminous sensation when describing light, and it means highly saturated when describing color.

COLOR CONTRASTS

The principles or effects of color contrasts determine how a color is perceived, how a color scheme is developed, and how objects are highlighted or partially concealed.

Since the three attributes of color are hue, saturation, and lightness, it is easy to identify the three basic contrasts: hue contrast, saturation contrast, and lightness contrast. What is red cannot be green; a strong green is not a weak green; a light blue is not a dark blue. Within these aspects alone, countless possibilities exist for effectively achieving a desired result.

Exploration of these contrasts provides a good basis for proficient color design; detailed study and practical experimentation are essential. Insufficient knowledge increases the risk of unpleasant visual and aesthetic consequences. Contrast effects may be helpful or harmful, and they are always present in the environment in one form or another. Here are some general hints:

1. Hues similar in saturation and value can unify a room and make a space seem larger. However, be sure to avoid monotony.
2. Contrast between walls and furnishings will make the furnishings more prominent.
3. Hue, value, and saturation contrast emphasize contours.
4. Visual spaciousness increases when similar colors are carried from one room to another.

Successive Contrast

If your eye becomes adapted to a particular hue by staring at it for some time, and then you shift your gaze to a white (or gray) surface, the complementary color will appear upon that surface. A white surface will look pale green, for example, after your eye has first adapted to a red stimulus. This is referred to as the afterimage phenomenon.

The afterimages are understood as a fatigue effect. As the cones in the retina adapt to a particular color, let us say red, the red-sensitive photoreceptors will be temporarily fatigued, and as the red stimulus is replaced by white, they respond less strongly to all the light rays reflected from the white surface. Only those sensitive to green will function fully.

The effect is not permanent, but the color patch that seems to float in front of the eyes can be disturbing and even annoying. This is especially true when performing tasks that require the eye to fixate continuously upon objects of the same color. This point may be illustrated by a case history involving a pharmaceutical factory.

Factory production-line workers, assigned to check purple pills, complained of migraines and of seeing green spots in front of their eyes. The problem was eliminated by surrounding the employees with green screens, against which the spots did not show. Company management had realized that green was the afterimage of purple-red, and therefore the green spots were the afterimage of the color of the pills.

To illustrate the point further, we can go back to the days when operating rooms in hospitals were white, as were the cover sheets and surgical gowns. Surgeons working at a strongly illuminated operating table were disturbed by the afterimages of blood and tissue that appeared when they would look temporarily at the white walls or the white gowns of their colleagues. Today, most gowns, cover sheets, and walls are green or blue-green, and the problem has been nearly eliminated.

The physiological fact is that the eye requires any given color to be balanced by its complementary, and will generate it if it is not present. Complementary colors, besides being psychological pairs in the eyes, provide a psychological balance of warmth and coolness of color. There is a strong tendency for people to seek a balance between warm and cool hues unconsciously.

Louis Cheskin, former associate director of the now defunct

Color Research Institute of America, related an experiment with three rooms in green. One room was treated in a single green, which gave rise to negative reactions. It was speculated that this response was due to uniformity, which now can be affirmed by the principle of unity and complexity balance. The second room, in three values of green, was considered neither favorable nor unfavorable. The third room, in three values of green, also had the complementary color of one of the values of the green (wine red), and reactions were 94 percent favorable. It may be argued that other factors could have contributed to the results, but the findings coincide with similar observations we have made.

The physiological phenomenon of afterimage is often used as proof that complementary colors are the basis of harmonious design. Also, when complementary colors are placed next to each other, the effect is both stimulating and pleasing because the afterimage of one enhances the other. A predominantly orange room, for instance, should have spots of complementary blue.

The concept of complementary hues is based on the color wheel, on which those colors that are diametrically opposite are considered complementary. In practice, it is impossible to seek technically *exact* complementaries, nor is it necessary. First of all, it is almost impossible to make an exact match among the standard paint colors, wallcoverings, and upholstery fabrics that a designer has to work with. Second, exact matches would limit overall color design considerations. The often-quoted maxim that true complementaries must mix or spin to gray may be filed away under things that are good to know but hard to do.

Simultaneous Contrast

Rarely is a color seen in isolation; in the visual field, different colors usually are seen simultaneously. This creates an optical effect closely related to successive contrast (afterimage). The eye will generate the complementary of the hue that it is seeing and project it toward the color adjacent to or superimposed upon it. The French chemist M. Chevreul, director of the Gobelins tapestry firm during the nineteenth century, called this effect *simultaneous contrast*, experimented extensively with it, and applied his findings to the weaving of tapestries.

The effect can be demonstrated by a simple experiment. Place a neutral gray square on a surrounding red background, and notice that the gray is tinged with green (the complementary of red) or appears greenish. Simultaneous contrast occurs not only between gray and a strong colored background, but also between any two hues (as long as they are not complementary). Each of the two hues tends to shift the other toward its own complement. Achromatic simultaneous contrast will make a gray appear dark against a light background, yet light against a dark background.

The effect of simultaneous contrast is more pronounced when the background color is saturated, and when it completely surrounds the surface being contrasted. Other observations show that closely related hues will lose some of their brightness, while complementary colors adjoining each other become intensified. Simultaneous contrasts are not as dramatic, or actually diminish, when a high contrast in brightness (light-dark contrast) exists between the colors.

COLOR HARMONIES AND COMBINATIONS

Traditionally, colors were chosen in terms of definite harmonious color schemes. Today, many designers reject rigid rules in favor of more freedom of artistic expression. Both camps have been able to argue their cases effectively. We, however, are more concerned with the psychological and physiological effects of colors in the environment than with personal artistic statements. In environments in which work must be performed, people's welfare must be considered, and learning must occur, the role of color is more than merely to entertain the senses.

Nonetheless, the functional role of color must also include beauty. It can never be assumed that beauty is unnecessary for mental well-being. Beauty or pleasantness might be an elusive element, however; what one person may consider beautiful, another may question. But there are color schemes that are pleasant and satisfying, just as there are unpleasant or discordant ones. In general, people react favorably to harmonious surroundings, and few people are completely oblivious to discord.

Awareness of traditional color harmonies is useful in understanding why certain colors work together and why some do not. The fact that they are considered too rigid by some colorists is surprising; it would be quite a task to exhaust all their possibilities. Color harmonies fall into two broad categories, related and contrasting. Related harmonies are subdivided into monochromatic and analogous. Contrasting color harmonies unite hues that are separated on the color wheel. The most common of these harmonies is the complementary color scheme.

Monochromatic harmonies are based on one hue varied in value and saturation—for example, pale green with pure green and dark green. With regard to interior design, there is real danger of monotony in such an arrangement. Used as a background for brighter tones of other colors, this scheme may serve a good purpose, but the overall color arrangement then ceases to be a true monochromatic harmony.

Analogous or related harmonies combine usually no more than three colors next to each other on the color wheel. The three hues are unified because of a shared color—for instance, red, yellow-red, and yellow; green, blue-green, and blue. Analogous color schemes offer more variety than monochromatic ones, but neither type will satisfy the problem of the afterimage phenomenon described earlier.

Complementary schemes are based on hues directly opposite each other on the color wheel. Examples are red and blue-green; yellow-red and blue; purple-blue and yellow. These harmonies offer more contrast and introduce both warm and cool colors into the environment. Careful handling of value and intensity, as with all contrasting schemes, is a prerequisite to ensure the success of these combinations.

Analogous-complementary is a term that could be used to describe a modification of the complementary scheme. This harmony is achieved by choosing two colors next to each other and combining them with the complementary of one of the two—for example, yellow-red and yellow combined with blue, the complementary of yellow-red.

Split-complementary harmony consists of one color and the two colors adjoining its complementary color. For instance, the complementary of red is blue-green, which is bordered by blue and green. The arrangement therefore would comprise red, blue, and green.

Double-complementary schemes recommend the use of two closely related hues and their complements. One example would be yellow-red and yellow with blue and purple-blue.

Other systematic variations of color relationships that are considered harmonious are triads and tetrads. *Triads* use three colors as equally spaced as possible on the color wheel, while *tetrads* are any four hues equidistant from each other.

According to the traditional school of colorists, complementary colors produce harmony and balance. According to the modern school of colorists, noncomplementary colors produce asymmetry and tension. *Asymmetric harmony* is based on two or more colors from one side of the color wheel without any shared hue. As with any asymmetric design, this creates tension. Then there is the *eclectic* approach, which uses neither of these two orientations. Here the selection of color is not based on complementary or noncomplementary color systems, or any rules, but rather on the colorist's personal interpretation of what may be appropriate for a given situation. This also often leads to asymmetry.

It is difficult to pass judgment on the asymmetric or eclectic approach without examining actual combinations. This holds true for any of the color harmony systems, since so much depends on their area (amount), value, and intensity relationships. Yet, there is one fact that should not be overlooked by practitioners of the asymmetric/eclectic school: When it comes to those interior environments that are discussed in this book, the uses of these two methods are limited. This should be obvious from the very word *tension*, which creates environmental conditions that are contrary to many of the psychophysiological principles we discuss.

COLOR SYSTEMS

Anyone working seriously with color will find it necessary to use some kind of color classification and order system. Color systems are an aid to composition, and they bring order into the confusion of the color range. In this way, colors are presented in sequence and in their relationship to each other, and they are listed neatly by hue, saturation, lightness, and interval.

Unfortunately, no international system has yet been established. Almost every major industrial nation has its own color standard, and most industries in which color is important have developed their own systems—none of which are interchangeable. The Commission Internationale de l'Eclairage (C.I.E.) has devised a color system based on spectrophotometric measurements of color samples, and it is the last word in accuracy. But for everyday practical use, it is not as convenient as those systems composed of color chips or patches with which a sample can be matched visually. C.I.E. specifications are presented in mathematical form, so it is necessary to refer to color samples built up from coordinates.

Most systems classify colors in terms of hue, lightness, and saturation. Some systems describe colors by their color content, referring to the proportion of white, black, or full color contained in a particular hue. (A full color is one considered to be highly saturated and at the same time as light as possible.)

Munsell System (*Munsell Book of Color*)

One of the most widely used methods of color notation is the Munsell system, which is explained here in some detail. Other systems are reviewed only briefly, not because they are of lesser value, but because the color specification tables in this book are based on Munsell notation.

Munsell colors are identified in terms of three attributes: hue, value (lightness), and chroma (saturation). Chosen so that the colors appear equally spaced, the Munsell system is based on five principal and five intermediate hues. Arranged clockwise around the color wheel by name (abbreviated by initials), they are: red (R), yellow-red (YR), yellow (Y), green-yellow (GY), green (G), blue-green (BG), blue (B), purple-blue (PB), purple (P), and red-purple (RP). Each named hue is subdivided further into four sections and designated 2.5, 5, 7.5, and 10, followed by its hue initial (2.5R, 5R, 7.5R, 10R). These are shown in the inner circle of the color wheel and may be used for rough identification of hue. Each named color is also divided into ten sections denoted by the numerals 1 to 100 and shown on the outer circle of the color wheel. These are used primarily for statistical records, cataloging, and computer programming.

The second dimension of the Munsell system is the value notation, indicating the degree of lightness or darkness of a color in relation to a neutral gray scale. The scale extends from absolute black (value symbol 0) to absolute white (value symbol 10). The symbol 5/ designates the middle value for gray and all chromatic colors that appear halfway in value between black and white. A green, for example, with the notation 9/ would be a light green; with the notation 3/, a dark green.

Chroma, or saturation, indicating strength or purity of color, is the third of the Munsell dimensions. Chroma notation is given from

/0 for a neutral gray to /10, /14, or /16, depending upon the saturation of a particular color.

Through this method, a color is identified by its three attributes (hue, value, chroma) instead of by limited and ambiguous names indicating vague identity, such as sky blue, primrose yellow, or mint green. The Munsell notation for a chromatic color is written in symbols showing its hue, value, and chroma position. For instance, a pink of moderate strength might be indicated as 5R 8/4 (5R = hue position, 8 = value, 4 = chroma).

The three Munsell color dimensions can be visualized in terms of a color space. The central vertical axis is the neutral-value gray scale, graded in equal visual steps from black to white. The hue scale, also in equal visual steps, is positioned around the neutral gray axis. Chroma scales radiate in equal visual steps outward from the neutral axis to the periphery of the color space.

The *Munsell Book of Color* is offered in two collections of 1,490 and 1,270 color chips, and there is a variety of other products available. Computer programs that convert C.I.E. data to Munsell color notations are available from the Rensselaer Color Measurement Laboratory, Rensselaer Polytechnic Institute, Troy, New York.

Ostwald System

Whereas the Munsell system identifies its colors by hue, value, and chroma, Ostwald is concerned with hue, white content, and black content. The color wheel is divided into twenty-four sections; the colors of the "cold" half of the circle—from yellow through green to blue—have been selected in such a way that they are complementary to those of the "warm" half—from blue through red to yellow. The eight principal hues are designated as follows: yellow, orange, red, purple, blue, turquoise, sea green, and leaf green. In Ostwald's color atlas, colors relating to each hue are arranged proportionally as formal triangles.

SIS Color Atlas

This atlas is based on the Swedish Natural Color System (NCS). It has been termed *natural* because it is based on Ewald Hering's psychophysical classifications of color in accordance with his six elementary color sensations: red, yellow, green, blue, white, and black. The colors in this system are classified by the attributes of hue, black content, and full color content. The color wheel is divided into four basic sections of yellow, red, blue, and green, with nine intermediate hues between each two basic colors. The notations are derived from the four hues plus whiteness and blackness. Approximately 1,300 colors in forty hues and five gray scales (achromatic, yellowish-, reddish-, bluish-, and greenish-grays) are available.

DIN Color Chart

The colors in the Deutsches Institut für Normung (DIN) system are classified by the attributes of hue, saturation, and relative lightness. The concept of relative lightness is defined as the relation between the color's lightness as perceived by a viewer and its greatest lightness at the same saturation and hue. The color wheel is divided into twenty-four sections with four basic hues (yellow, green, blue, red). Approximately 600 or 900 colors in twenty-four hues and an achromatic scale are available.

The preceding four color systems are some of the best known but not the only ones in existence. An excellent overview of these four and many others appears in the book *Color in Townscape* (Düttman et al. 1981). The *Munsell Book of Color* is available from Munsell Color, 2441 North Calvert Street, Baltimore, Maryland 21218; the *SIS Color Atlas* from SIS-Standardiseringskommissionen i Sverige, Stockholm, Sweden, or Skandinaviska Färginstitutet, Stockholm, Sweden; the *DIN Color Chart* from Beuth Verlag GmbH, Burggrafenstrasse 4, 1000 Berlin 30, East Germany.

Paint Color Systems

Almost every designer and architect works with one or more paint systems in specifying interior or exterior colors. All paint manufacturers have their own color systems related to their standard or custom-mixed colors. Most of these are adequate for their purposes; some are more elaborate than others. They should not be confused, however, with the color specification systems discussed previously. In many cases, written identification is made for hue, and colors usually are presented in some order in regard to chroma and value.

But no written or symbolic notation is given for a color's saturation and lightness, so visual judgments must be made. This is fine, as long as the colors selected for a particular project come from the same paint manufacturer.

One system's superiority over another depends on the variety and amount of colors available, how the system is organized to facilitate design work, and the designer's individual preference. The general organization (not specifics) of paint color systems can be explained through one of the more elaborate types available. This is the Glidden Professional Colors arrangement produced by SCM Glidden Coating & Resins, Cleveland, Ohio. The color specification tables in this book (along with Munsell) are based on Glidden colors, and the color collages were made with Glidden color samples.

The Professional Colors system provides a selector book of 1,024 interior colors arranged in the following color sequence: off-white/warm tones, off-white/cool tones, red/red-violet, red, red-orange, orange, orange-yellow, yellow-orange, yellow, yellow/yellow-green, muted yellow-green, yellow-green, green, green/blue-green, blue-green, blue-green/blue, blue, blue/blue-violet, blue-violet, violet, light brown/brown, gray, and accent colors. With the exception of white and accent colors, each individual hue section contains colors in systematic gradations of saturation and lightness.

The complete system contains the selector book and a fan deck that matches it, as well as two volumes of color sheets, each sheet containing nine removable chips. Individual colors are identified in numerical sequence from 70-01 for the first off-white sample to 80-24 for the last accent-color sample. Light-reflection percentages are also indicated on each color sample.

Vision and Light

Vision, the richest human sense, provides us with a wealth of information we would not receive without light—the basic stimulus for vision. Both have a decisive influence upon our reactions, ability to concentrate, efficiency, fatigue, and general well-being. The ability of the eyes to function on an optimum level is in direct relationship to light. Therefore, light and the environment where it is to be installed have to adapt themselves to the physiological laws of vision.

THE OPTICAL SYSTEM

Since the eyes and light work directly together, environmental design applications demand a fundamental knowledge of the human optical system. A brief review follows.

The Structure of the Eye

Basically, the eye consists of the cornea, the iris, the lens, and the retina. The cornea, which serves as a preliminary lens helping to focus light, is the transparent covering in front of the eye. Incoming light enters the cornea and passes through the pupil, the opening in

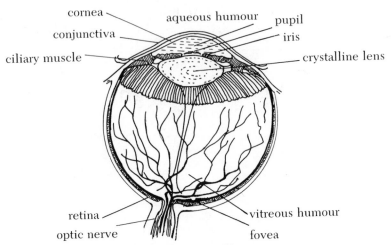

Schematic drawing of human eye.

the center of the eye. The amount of light admitted through the pupil is controlled by a ring of muscles called the iris (whose pigmentation determines the eye's color). The path continues through the lens, which modifies its curvature to focus the light so that it produces a clear image on the retina.

The retina, the inner surface of the eye, is an intricate network of receptor cells and neurons where light is converted into neural impulses that are forwarded to the brain. The retina contains two types of photoreceptor cells—rods and cones. In dim light, the rods (about 120 million in one eye) react to brightness but not to color. Rods contain rhodopsin, a photopigment that is much more light-sensitive than are photopigments in the cones. Thus, rods can operate in dim light when cones become useless. The cones (about six million in one eye) operate in increased light and are responsible for detailed vision and color perception. Rods predominate in the peripheral regions of the retina, whereas cones are concentrated in the central region of the retina. Cones are the only receptors in the very center of the retinal area that lies almost directly opposite the pupil—the fovea. The fovea is the region of most distinct or detailed vision.

After photochemically registering the presence of light, the rods and cones pass their electrical potential through bipolar cells to ganglion cells. The axons of ganglion cells form the optic nerve, which relays visual information to the brain. When the brain responds to these impulses and analyzes the message it has received, we begin to see.

Color Vision

Many aspects of color vision still are not well understood. Among the several theories proposed are the opponent-process theory, the retinex theory, and the trichromatic theory. The trichromatic theory is perhaps the major one. First advanced in the nineteenth century by Thomas Young and elaborated by Herman von Helmholtz, it proposes that color vision is based on three types of cones, each type most sensitive to wavelengths of red, green, or blue respectively. All colors are seen through combinations of them.

The Eye Muscles

The eye has both internal and external muscles. The external muscles direct the eyes to a point of interest, and they work together to keep both eyes centered upon it. Internal muscles control focusing and pupil size.

The process by which the eye changes focus from one distance to another is called *accommodation*. To change focus, the shape of the lens must change, which involves the ciliary muscle. This muscle is connected to an elastic ring of suspensory ligaments (zonula) around the lens of the eye. In its resting state, the eye is set for distant vision; the ciliary muscle is relaxed and the suspensory ligaments are tense. When a near object is to be viewed, the ciliary muscle contracts to reduce the tension on the suspensory ligaments, thereby changing the curvature of the lens. The ciliary muscle must exert a continuous contracting force to maintain focus on a near object.

Adaptation is the immediate reaction of the eye to changes in the degree of illumination or brightness. The widening or narrowing of the pupil size is accomplished by the tiny muscles in the iris. The cones in the retina become active in a change to bright light, and the rods become active in a change to dim light.

THE ENVIRONMENT AND AGREEABLE VISUAL CONDITIONS

The question of how much light is needed for clear and comfortable vision has been belabored for many years by illuminating engineers. The subject of too much versus too little light is a matter of constant debate. Too little light will handicap vision and too much will overtax it. The technical engineering of lighting installations usually is out of the hands of the designer, but he or she does have control over the relationship between light and the quality of the visual environment.

In the design of the environmental space, concern must be shown for conditions that will affect visual efficiency and comfort. It is often assumed that eye fatigue is a matter of retinal nerve fatigue; this is not so. The retina seems more or less immune to fatigue and can take much stress. It is muscles, not eye nerves, that are likely to cause trouble. Just like any muscle subjected to excessive activity, eye muscles will tire. Glare, constant adjustment to extreme brightness differences, prolonged fixation of the eyes, and constant shifts in accommodation will tire eyes quickly, causing headaches, tension, nausea, and other disturbances.

It is essential to control extreme contrasts in light and dark. If these contrasts are not regulated, the iris muscles experience undue stress because the pupil is forced to undergo constant adjustment. E. Grandjean of the Institute for Industrial Hygiene and Work Physiology in Zurich, reports on a study where properly controlled brightness contrasts in a work environment significantly increased performance and decreased physiological fatigue.

Vision should be held at midtones, an ideal light-to-reflection ratio being 3:1. This means controlling the light-reflection ratios of walls, furniture, desks, and floors. Recommended reflectances for surfaces are 20 percent for floors, 25 to 40 percent for furniture, 40 to 60 percent for walls (which can be stretched to 70 percent in certain cases), and 80 to 90 percent for ceilings. Insufficient or feeble contrasts are emotionally unsatisfying and should be avoided.

Glare also puts debilitating strain on the eyes. Direct glare results from insufficiently shielded light sources, the extreme being bare bulbs. Unshaded windows can also cause direct glare. Individuals should be situated so that they do not face windows. Window walls should always be light in color to eliminate strong brightness contrasts between dark walls and the entering sunlight. Reflected glare results from specular reflection of high luminances on polished surfaces. This is one of the reasons that matte work surfaces and walls are highly recommended.

Light sources, whether of high or low intensity, always should be properly baffled with louvers or lenses. For work tasks demanding a great deal of light, a localized light source may be introduced, but this should never be done in an otherwise-dark room.

LIGHT'S EFFECT ON COLOR

Careful control of color is as important for an agreeable environment as are brightness controls. On a practical basis, this means one of two things. Either color is adjusted to an environment's existing lights (which is the less desirable, since they might be changed) or color and lights are specified simultaneously. Depending on a light's spectral distribution in the visible region, color shifts do occur, and some lights render colors better than others. What is also involved is the color of the light itself. For example, is it a warm light or a cool one?

Observations made by A.A. Kruithof in 1941 are worth noting here. He found that people prefer a cool color temperature when illumination is intense and a warmer color temperature when illumination is low. He also reported that objects and surfaces will have a normal color appearance under warm light at low intensity and under cool light at high intensity.

It is crucial to understand the spectral quality of artificial light in order to know how it will affect color, so a brief explanation follows. (Biological concerns related to spectral quality are discussed in chapter 6.)

Spectral Power Distribution

The amount of power from a light source in each color band or spectral region is called spectral power distribution (SPD). For instance, the energy output of the standard cool-white fluorescent lamp is concentrated in the yellow-green region of the spectrum, where the eye is more sensitive to brightness. This was designed to maximize achromatic visibility, thus making it quite different from natural light, which has a more even distribution. Other features can be determined from the SPD.

Color Rendering Index

The color rendering index (CRI) was developed to describe how well colors (including the appearances of people) are rendered by artificial light sources compared to natural light. It must be emphasized that this is a measure of how a light source compares with natural light at a specific *correlated color temperature*. High-CRI lamps provide illumination that affects the color of objects in the same way that natural light does. Phases of natural light vary according to such factors as season, time of day, and weather, and these different phases result in color temperatures measured by degrees Kelvin (K). Any source can give a cool cast to colors if its correlated color temperature is high, or a warm cast if it is low. Therefore, the CRI should never be used without relating it to the correlated color temperature.

The CRI measure for natural outdoor light is 100. The higher the CRI of a lamp (also taking into account the color of the light source itself), the more it renders colors in the environment as "true." In other words, spectral distribution of the visible light region is less distorted. Full-spectrum light sources, for instance, have a CRI of over 90, cool white 68, warm white 56, and some of the energy-saving types of lights approximately 48.

Color Temperature

The term *color temperature* was devised to describe the color of light emitted by a natural source. The term refers to the temperature in degrees Kelvin at which a blackbody (a theoretically perfect radiator) would have to be heated to match the perceived color of the light source. To simplify, when the old-time blacksmith heated a piece of iron, the iron started to glow a deep red. As it got hotter, its color changed gradually until it finally became "white hot." The easiest way to describe the color of glowing metal is to give its temperature.

Color temperature applies only to natural sources (sun, sky, incandescent metal sources). When referring to light sources, such as fluorescent, mercury, and other arcs, the proper term is *correlated color temperature*. A warm-white fluorescent may have a correlated color temperature of 3000°K, giving it the appearance of a warm light (orange glow). Daylight fluorescent at 6500°K will cast a cooler light (bluish glow).

Biological Effects of Light

For years, the lighting industry adhered to the belief that the only significant role of light is to provide adequate illumination, that it should be an aid in "seeing." Although lamps were developed with efficient light emission, they left great gaps in the full spectrum found in sunlight.

During the last two decades, it has become increasingly clear that sunlight (natural global solar radiation) has a profound effect on the human organism. As Küller stated:

> The reason for this is firstly that solar radiation was important for the genesis of life itself, actually without light there would be no life. The second reason is that the development of higher life and man to this day occurred under the constant influence of solar radiation affecting living tissue from the single cell of the skin to the specially adapted light-sensitive eye. Thus the amount of light, the quality of light, the distribution of light and the variation of light between day and night and winter and summer are closely tied to the genesis of man and we are gaining better understanding of some of these ties (Küller 1981, 9).

For nearly a century, the human organism has been subjected to electric light. The spectrum of the incandescent bulb does not differ too much from that of natural light in the visible light region,

43

but it emits very little ultraviolet radiation. Because of its low color temperature, incandescent light is a warm illumination closely resembling fire, candle, kerosene lamp, and gas mantle light. Nowadays, used primarily as residential illumination, it fits into the spectral exposure history of humans—natural light during the daytime and fire (warm light) at night. Some adaptive effects might be evident, at least psychologically, since warm light is associated with relaxation.

Fluorescent light, introduced on a large scale in the late 1940s, is potentially of far greater significance biologically, mainly for two reasons: First, its spectral composition differs markedly from that of natural light, and second, it has replaced natural light during the daytime for a large majority of the population. Artificial light, however, although an efficient optic substitute, is not a substitute for natural light in physiological terms.

Today, with more understanding of the effects of natural light (sunlight), the emphasis in artificial light is shifting from vision alone to biological needs. Research indicates that constant exposure to ordinary artificial light has biological implications. If sunlight is normal, artificial light is subnormal or abnormal. If sunlight, the balanced light, is essential for the growth and health of living things, including man, it seems logical to raise questions about the effects that unbalanced (artificial) light may have on life, including the human organism. Answers to these questions have been the goal of many investigators. One of these is John Ott, renowned for his research work on the influence of light and color on plants, animals, and man.

A pioneer in the field of time-lapse photography, Ott shot sequences of flowers and plants and noticed that periodicity, intensity, and wavelength distribution of light energy control plant growth processes. He observed that too much exposure to artificial light had adverse effects, and this raised questions in his mind about the effects of light upon animals. Subsequent experiments with rats showed that their growth and health also were affected adversely by excessive exposure to nonnatural light. Included in these findings was the fact that rats developed various aberrant behavior patterns, including hyperactivity.

All this caused Ott to wonder whether light might have effects on the basic physiology of human beings. In 1966, the Environmental Health and Light Research Institute of Sarasota, Florida, was established under Ott's directorship. His multifaceted studies (the result of a lifetime of investigation), many of which have been substantiated by other scientific research, point to the fact that light, whether natural or artificial, has a profound effect on the human organism. As Ott pointed out:

> We know that every chemical, mineral, vitamin, or substance of any kind that we take into our bodies as food has a maximum wavelength absorption characteristic of electromagnetic energy. We also know that this wavelength energy penetrates the skin and interacts directly at the molecular level with the chemicals and minerals in the blood supply (Ott 1981, 21).

This conclusion may be exemplified by the medical use of light radiation for curative purposes in infant jaundice (hyperbilirubinemia). Accepted treatment for this condition is the use of blue light, which passes through the tissue and interacts with and breaks down the bilirubin serum in the blood so that it can be excreted.

Physiological effects of light are not confined to radiation on the skin, nor is light entering the eye confined to the stimulation of vision. Ott explained further:

> We also know that light received through the eyes stimulates the pineal and pituitary glands. These glands control the endocrine system that regulates the production and release of hormones controlling body chemistry. This would then seem to me to be a carry-over of the basic principles of photosynthesis in plants—sometimes referred to as a conversion of light energy into chemical energy—to animal life, a phenomenon not heretofore recognized. Thus the wavelengths that are missing in various types of artificial light or that are filtered from the spectrum of natural light by window glass, windshields, eyeglasses (particularly tinted contact lenses or deeper shades of sunglasses), smog, and even suntan lotions, are causing a condition of malillumination, similar to the malnutrition that occurs when there is a lack of a proper nutritional diet.
>
>   Those minerals and chemicals in the individual cells of our bodies that would normally be metabolized by the wavelengths that are missing remain in the equivalent of darkness, even though other wavelengths are present. The end result is an incomplete metabolic or biological combustion process (Ott 1981, 25).

In 1984, The New York Academy of Sciences presented a conference on medical and biological effects of light. The conference announcement explained their goals:

Environmental light produces numerous biological effects related to health beyond simply affecting vision and cutaneous pigmentation. Some of these involve direct responses of circulating or cutaneous chemicals to light waves; others are mediated by the brain and neuroendocrine organs. The sufficient excellent work that now exists warrants a conference that focuses on recent advances in the understanding of these effects—effects that may be important for the design of interior environments that optimize health.

For practical purposes, we will not concern ourselves here with the full extent of electromagnetic energy, but rather with visible light and the adjacent infrared and ultraviolet regions. These three components of solar radiation will affect the human organism in two ways—through radiation on the skin and light entering the eye. Some of these effects, besides stimulating vision, may be summarized thus:

Ultraviolet Radiation
Actinic effects on the skin
Erythema (reddening of the skin)
Vitamin D production
Physiological effects of a general nature

Light Radiation (Visible Light)
Activation of pineal organ
Endocrine and autonomic effects
Entrainment of circadian rhythms
Effects on performance and fatigue
Cognitive, behavioral, and emotional correlates

Infrared Radiation
Heating action on the skin
Vasodilation
Influence on body temperature
Influence on physical and mental performance (through body temperature)
Cold, heat, and pain sensations

ULTRAVIOLET RADIATION

Exposure to ultraviolet (UV) radiation is a matter of controversy these days. One school of thought warns of health risks and therefore does not see sufficient reason for the inclusion of UV radiation in the category of artificial light. The other school of thought believes that trace amounts of the radiation in artificial light are necessary, especially for those people who spend most of their time indoors.

There is no doubt that overexposure to ultraviolet radiation can be harmful. It may cause reddening of the skin (erythema), give rise to a variety of photoallergies, and cause skin cancer. Yet, UV radiation is also essential to human welfare, and by completely protecting ourselves from any trace amounts, we risk creating a deficiency in this life-supporting energy.

Ultraviolet radiation is considered to be in the wavelength range of 100 to 400 nanometers (nm = one millionth of a millimeter). Specific wavelength bands often are designated by different notations, such as UV-A, near-ultraviolet, or black light. This often leads to confusion (see table 1). For convenience, we will refer to the system used frequently by photobiologists. This subdivides UV radiation into three bands, UV-A (from 315 to 400 nm), UV-B (from 280 to 315 nm), and UV-C (from 100 to 280 nm).

Several processes that go on in the skin depend on the photochemical (actinic) effect of UV radiation. One of these is the synthesis of calciferol, or vitamin D. Vitamin D, which promotes the metabolism of phosphorus and calcium in the body, is produced by the UV radiation in the B range, which also has the erythemal and pigmenting effect on the human skin. Deficiency might result in rickets or dental caries in children, or brittle bones in the aged.

Ordinary window glass will absorb essentially all UV-B radiation. Ultraviolet of the A range passes through most types of glass but produces virtually no vitamin D or erythema. UV-A, however, can cause erythema when the skin has been subjected to the action of drugs that make it abnormally light-sensitive. UV-C radiation has a strong germicidal effect, and it may cause superficial erythema.

It is commonly held that only small amounts of ultraviolet radiation are needed to help develop calciferol. Rickets, for example, can be cured by repeated exposure to one-tenth the dose of UV required to obtain reddening of the skin. R.M. Neer (1971) pointed out that the amount of radiation involved is roughly the equivalent of exposure to UV radiation that a Washington, D.C., resident might receive during a fifteen-minute midsummer lunchtime stroll. It appears, then, that reasonable exposure to sunlight and intake of dietary vitamin D would be sufficient preventive measures. However, ultraviolet radiation can also have physiological effects of a general nature, which are discussed later in this chapter.

Vitamin D deficiency among the elderly tends to be a matter of concern. Elderly people who often stay indoors, especially during the winter months, or who are institutionalized and eat poorly, may run the risk of simultaneous reduction in both cutaneous and dietary vitamin D. The 1979 study by Lawson, Paul, and Cole concludes that the vitamin D condition of the elderly may reach levels associated with osteomalacia (soft bones) in winter.

Neer and some associates conducted a study among elderly residents of the Chelsea (Massachusetts) Soldiers' Home during two consecutive winters (Neer et al. 1971). It was found that intestinal calcium absorption increased among subjects exposed to a fluorescent lamp designed to duplicate daylight, and decreased in the control group exposed to conventional cool-white fluorescent. After dairy products in the institution were fortified with vitamin D, the same results were obtained.

Although definite conclusions cannot be drawn in view of the few studies conducted, it is possible that vitamin D deficiency may also cause an increase in dental caries. In 1974, R.P. Feller and associate investigators exposed cotton rats variously to incandescent, cool-white fluorescent, and simulated sunlight illumination. They found that the incidence of caries was significantly higher in those rats housed under cool-white fluorescent than those under the other two light sources. Sharon, Feller, and Burney (1971) found that golden hamsters exposed to light simulating the visible and UV spectra of natural light had one-fifth as many caries as those exposed to standard fluorescent illumination. L.W. Mayron et al. (1974) studied schoolchildren in two classrooms, one lighted by cool-white fluorescent and the other by full-spectrum lamps. The incidence and the extent of caries among the cool-white group were significantly higher than among the full-spectrum group.

Research suggests that UV radiation might also have general physiological effects, such as a decrease in pulse rate, a drop in blood pressure, changes in skin temperature and metabolic rate, a reduction in reaction time, an improvement in health conditions, and resistance to certain types of infections. Studies by E.F. Ellinger (using the bicycle-ergometer) have indicated that exposure of human subjects to erythema-producing doses of UV radiation resulted in an improved work output due to decreased fatigability and increased efficiency (Ellinger, quoted in Birren 1982). M.A. Zamkova and E.I. Krivitskaya (1966) were able to show in their experiments that subjects irradiated with UV radiation had a shorter reaction time to light and sound, a lower fatigability of the visual receptors, and an improvement in working capacity. During these experiments, which were conducted with schoolchildren, the investigators found that the subjects' academic standing also improved, probably due to these favorable shifts.

The U.S.S.R. Academy of Medical Sciences has compiled extensive clinical data on the effects of ultraviolet radiation. These data point out that lack of exposure to sunlight, in addition to vitamin D deficiency and demineralization of bones and teeth, will result in a weakening of the body's immunological defenses and increased stress and fatigue. Research undertaken by MIT, NASA, Harvard, and others confirms these findings.

At the sixteenth meeting of the International Commission on Illumination, held in Washington, D.C., in 1967, Dantsig, Lazarev, and Sokolov of the U.S.S.R. reported positive clinical and physiological changes, a reduction in the incidence of diseases, and an increase in overall immunological responsiveness in children irradiated with UV radiation. They also noted that the majority of nonirradiated children showed a reduction in body defenses. Similarly, a study of children in a Swedish day-care center showed a clear-cut relationship between the duration of outdoor activity (therefore UV exposure) and resistance to respiratory infections. The three Russian scientists also stated: "The Institute of General and Community Hygiene under the U.S.S.R. Academy of Medical Sciences has taken a positive view of the effectiveness of utilizing erythemal lamps in the system of artificial lighting."

With regard to the Russian literature, Luke Thorington remarked:

> It is noteworthy that all of these reported effects are achieved through suberythemal dosages of ultraviolet—dosages delivered over an eight-hour day that are only one-tenth to about one-half of that required to produce the least perceptible skin reddening (Thorington 1973, 31–36).

There is also some evidence that UV radiation might affect muscle tone and strength. According to a report sent to John Ott from the National Institutes of Health in 1978, modest amounts of near–UV light increased shoulder muscle tone and improved short-term strength. Specific exclusion of near–UV light reduced muscle tone and strength. (Only shoulder muscles were tested.) Some studies by other investigators have also demonstrated increase of muscle strength when subjects are exposed to ultraviolet radiation.

Undoubtedly, more research still has to be done on the effects of ultraviolet radiation. So far, evidence indicates that there are definite health risks from overexposure, yet a modest amount of UV radiation seems to be a necessity.

A provocative, if not baffling, study on the incidence of skin cancer among Australians appeared in the August 7, 1982, medical journal *The Lancet*. Research conducted in England by the Department of Medical Statistics and Epidemiology, London School of Hygiene and Tropical Medicine, and in Australia by the University of Sydney and Melanoma Clinic, Sydney Hospital, found that "exposure to fluorescent light at work was associated with a doubling of melanoma risk." The risk of developing malignant melanomas grew with the increasing duration of exposure to fluorescent light and was higher in women who had worked mainly in offices than in women whose main place of work was not in offices yet still indoors. The report also mentioned that melanoma rates in Britain and Australia are higher among professionals and office workers and are lower in people working *outdoors*. If only one thing can be proven conclusively from this report, it is that there is a need for further research.

Millions of people work in buildings with windows that cannot be opened, or with no windows at all. Ordinary window glass absorbs essentially all of the "biologically active" ultraviolet spectra, and standard indoor incandescent and fluorescent lamps do not emit significant amounts of ultraviolet. The small amount that is emitted from fluorescent lights usually is absorbed by the fixtures on which they are mounted. Furthermore, these workers travel (especially in winter) to and from work in closed vehicles and usually venture outdoors only in early morning or late evening, when UV radiation is minimal. It appears that the use of artificial light that includes a modest amount of UV (as in full-spectrum lamps such as Vita-Lite) is justified, if not necessary in these cases.

INFRARED RADIATION

For all practical purposes, a detailed description of infrared action is somewhat superfluous here. Infrared is weak in fluorescent light sources but exists to a higher degree in energy emitted from incandescent lamps. Also, individuals have control to some extent over temperature regulation in their indoor environment. Nonetheless, infrared radiation is part of light, so it is worth discussing some of its basic aspects.

Light contains infrared energy that penetrates the skin and muscles, resulting in increased circulation of the blood. The primary action of infrared on the skin is that of heating. This generally leads to a vasodilation of cutaneous blood vessels, which in turn gives rise to a number of other reactions. If body temperature becomes excessively high (or low), the organism is alerted to restore balance. The hypothalamus is the primary center for the regulation of body temperature and metabolism. Needless to say, body temperature influences the performance of a wide variety of physical and mental activities.

PHYSIOLOGICAL EFFECTS OF NATURAL AND ARTIFICIAL LIGHT ENTERING THE EYE

Vision is not the only result of light entering the eye; it also induces biological functions in both animals and man. This occurs via a pathway independent of the visual process that F. Hollwich has described (1980) as the "energetic portion" of the visual pathway. The preface of his book *The Influence of Ocular Light Perception on Metabolism in Man and in Animals* introduced the idea:

> In experiments performed over a period of almost three decades (1948–1975), the author [Dr. Hollwich] and co-workers were the first to demonstrate conclusively that the eye is the channel for light's stimulatory effect. In order to elucidate this effect and separate it clearly from the visual process, in 1948 the author [Dr. Hollwich] designated the neural pathway conducting the photostimulus to the pituitary gland (hypophysis) as the "energetic portion" of the optic pathway. Vision itself proceeds independently via the "optic portion" of the optic pathway (Hollwich 1980).

This neural pathway seems to involve the hypothalamus, which monitors changes in the body's internal environment. It sends signals to the autonomic nervous system to respond to environmental changes, and it affects the production of hormones throughout the endocrine system by influencing the pituitary gland. Also affected by light is the pineal gland, involved in the synthesis and secretion of the hormone melatonin. Ott also remarked:

> In addition to the optic track and independent thereof, it is now well established that neurochemical channels connect a photoreceptor mechanism in the retina with both the pineal and pituitary glands and hypothalamic mid-brain region. The pineal and pituitary glands are the master glands that control the entire endocrine system, the production and release of hormones or, in other words, basic body chemistry (Ott 1979, 8).

Hollwich and colleagues studied the effect of strong artificial light with considerable deviation from the spectral composition, and, on the other hand, minimal deviation in healthy persons. In those persons subjected to light with the greater deviation, they found stresslike levels of ACTH (a hormone of the anterior part of the pituitary gland that stimulates the growth and hormone production of the adrenal cortex) and the stress hormone cortisol. Hollwich concluded that this explains the agitated mental and physical behavior of children who stay in school the whole day and are subjected to artificial illumination that deviates strongly from daylight. Mayron et al., in 1974, demonstrated that "full-spectrum fluorescent lighting" decreased the hyperactive behavior of students in two first-grade classrooms. The comparison was made between the full-spectrum light and standard cool-white fluorescent.

Hollwich, Dieckhues, and Schrameyer (1977) also found that increasing the intensity of artificial light with fluorescent tubes leads to "light stress." Proof of this was increased hormone production, especially of cortisol. The investigators noted that it is inappropriate from a medical point of view to believe that artificial light is the same as natural light and therefore can fully replace it.

The most obvious relationship between man and light is the light/dark (wakefulness/sleep) cycle of day and night and its complex physiological and biochemical variations. The timing of diurnal (daytime) and nocturnal (nighttime) rhythms and the functional variations related to them depends on internal processes, which can be referred to as the biological clock. There must be a synchronizer to keep time with sunrise and sunset. Richard Wurtman and associates have proposed the melatonin theory of pineal function. Melatonin is a hormone produced by the pineal body that regulates the activity of certain glands. It seems that the synthesis of melatonin in the pineal gland holds a central position in producing the effects of light received through the eyes.

Wurtman wrote: "The role of pineal cells appears to be to convert a neural input controlled by an exogenous factor (light) to an endogenous glandular output (its hormone)" (Wurtman 1969, 32). It is widely believed that environmental illumination controls the rate of melatonin synthesis.

It is also thought that melatonin affects the regulation of behavior changes in animals, but this has not been shown clearly in humans. In one study, drug-sized doses of melatonin given to volunteers produced a sedating effect; alertness, viligance, and reaction time declined.

In both animals and people, melatonin is turned off during the day (under sunlight) and released at night. Animals, however, respond to lower levels of light in melatonin suppression, while humans are unresponsive to even bright indoor lights. In 1982, Dr. Alfred Lewy et al. demonstrated that very bright light, in the morning and in the evening, could grant relief to a manic-depressive patient suffering from winter-long depression. People with winter depression, known as *seasonal affective disorder* (SAD), show symptoms of decreased physical activity, increased carbohydrate craving, decreased energy level, irritability, and sleep disorders. Melatonin may be the key chemical messenger in this disease.

Norman Rosenthal and associates (1984), using 2500 lux (the metric equivalent of footcandles) of white full-spectrum light, also found that artificial extension of the day, three hours before dawn and three hours after dusk, had an antidepressant effect upon patients. Although bright light seems to help alleviate the problems of certain depressives, this does not mean 2500 lux of light should be installed in every artificially lit environment in the winter. It is important to remember that the length of the day was changed in these cases.

It is obvious that man needs light, as Wurtman has stated: "It seems clear that light is the most important environmental input, after food, in controlling bodily functions" (quoted in Birren 1973). Yet we are using more light and for longer periods during the twenty-four-hour cycle than ever before. In doing so, we lose our connection to the diurnal and seasonal variations of natural light. The amount of light that people are subjected to now is very different from that at the turn of the century. We switch lights on in the morning (at least in the winter) and we use additional light in work spaces, at times adding even more to it for special tasks. In the evening, many of us go shopping in highly illuminated spaces and finally end up in front of a flickering television set. It might be time to ask whether this is too much light instead of whether it is enough.

The foregoing discussion was designed to instill a sense of caution in regard to the all-too-common belief that artificial light is only an aid in seeing. Clearly, there are significant differences between artificial light and natural light. The use of artificial light, which is more dominated by longer wavelengths than daylight, can disturb the pineal balance, and there is no doubt that stresslike reactions may be caused by artificial light if the spectrum deviates considerably—especially if it is flickering or glaring, or if it is intense.

ARTIFICIAL SUNLIGHT—WHEN AND WHERE?

Much research remains to be done before there are firm conclusions about the long-term effects of artificial light. In the meantime, it is important to be cautious in using all kinds of light sources as freely as we do. From a photobiological viewpoint, perhaps it would be better to move people back into full-spectrum illumination, particularly those people who spend their working day under the illumination of deficient spectra. This raises the question of where and when artificial full-spectrum light should be used.

At the present time, the authors are aware of only one patented general-purpose light source that simulates the balanced ultraviolet and full visible spectrum of natural daylight. That is Vita-Lite, manufactured by the Duro-Test Corporation, North Bergen, New Jersey. Many of the research studies discussed within this chapter either mentioned Vita-Lite or simply referred to full-spectrum light or light that simulates sunlight. This may indicate the possibility that other artificial full-spectrum lamps are available besides Vita-Lite.

Should full-spectrum lighting be recommended for every environment? A general answer of *yes* or *no* obviously cannot be given without knowledge of details of the nature of the environment. Any specific recommendation offered without consideration of the variables involved is arbitrary at best.

To make any suggestions regarding light, it is important to make an analysis of the environment:

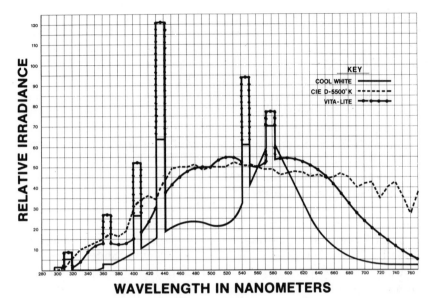

WAVELENGTH IN NANOMETERS

Spectral power distribution (SPD) chart of cool-white, CIE D-5500°K, and Vita-Lite (courtesy of Duro-Test Corporation).

1. What type of environment will it be?
2. What will its function be?
3. Who will inhabit it, for how long, doing what tasks?

There are situations in which full-spectrum light can be introduced into certain spaces and left out in others within the same environment. To illustrate the point: In schools, full-spectrum lighting should be used in classrooms, libraries, and gymnasiums, but it is not particularly necessary in corridors.

If a particular lighting situation demands the inclusion of UV radiation, it should by all means be included. If not, illumination with a high CRI rating should always be considered—not only on the basis of biological effects caused by illumination of distorted spectral composition (in the visible-light region), but also in regard to visual aspects.

Hughes and Neer (1981) have pointed out that a number of researchers have examined the significance of using high-CRI full-spectrum light, as opposed to standard cool-white sources, for illuminating living and work areas. It should be stressed that high-CRI lamps produce a subjective visual clarity much higher than that achieved by standard cool-white lamps. Based on visual clarity studies, lighting engineers in Europe recommend a minimum of CRI 85. In the United States, even the most widely used fluorescent lamps do not meet that CRI rating. Lemaigre-Voreaux demonstrated in 1970 that the high-CRI lamps not only produced better visual clarity, but about 750 lux of high-CRI lamps provided the same visual clarity and perceptual satisfaction in an environment as 1076 lux of a cool-white source (Lemaigre-Voreaux, quoted in Hughes and Neer 1981, 75).

Another consideration in evaluating full-spectrum light is that of visual acuity and fatigue. A study conducted in 1974 by Douglas Kleiber and associates at Cornell University demonstrated that Vita-Lite increased visual acuity and decreased general fatigue over a four-hour study period. According to tests conducted around 1984 by H.R. Blackwell, a vision expert at Ohio State University, lighting limited to a narrow band of the visible spectrum can diminish productivity. Full-spectrum lights greatly improve visual performance.

Some lighting applications do not require simulated sunlight. These may be where lights of a lower color temperature (warmer) are desired to induce various psychological effects, including relaxation. Examples would be employees' lounges or cafeterias (see chapter 13). Also, occasions arise in which human complexion needs to be flattered instead of being viewed as it normally appears.

There are many types of light sources on the market for almost any type of lighting conditions required. A little research into what is available, coupled with a careful analysis of what is required in the environment, will provide a workable solution.

SEVEN

Bioenergetics

The subject of bioenergetics has been researched for only a generation and is not yet fully understood by scientists. However, an emerging interest in it seems to indicate the need for an introduction to the subject. More than twenty periodicals are published in Austria, West Germany, and Switzerland on the discoveries of bioenergetic environments. In the United States, a company is starting to introduce and build environments based on bioenergetic developments.

Bioenergetics as a general study is not within our professional expertise, except as it relates to light. Therefore, this chapter merely presents a subject of interest (as a newspaper might do), leaving the luxury of personal opinion or professional analysis, whichever the case may be, to the reader.

The following discussion of this subject is a condensed version of the pamphlet *A New Dimension for a Healthy Environment Comes to America—Discoveries in Bio-Energetics*, by Walter R.G. Kumpe. The authors have taken the liberty of making some modifications to ensure continuity.

Let us first discuss briefly the discoveries of bioenergetic research. *Bioenergy* refers to all natural electric, magnetic, light, and other energies that together make up the cosmic background and earth radiations that are absorbed by and affect all life. Like heart and breath, all aspects of life pulsate continually, expand and contract, implode and explode, in a polarized natural rhythm. Ancient Chinese named this universal polarity yin and yang, and today scientists are discovering this same pulsation principle in everything from the level of atoms to that of giant quasars millions of light-years away. Proper polarization—positive and negative charges in balance—maintains an organism in health and harmony with its environment.

Practically, polarization refers to the vital ability to absorb, assimilate, and distribute energy. The healthy heart is an excellent example of this. In its relaxed state, the heart allows the blood to be drawn to it from the various parts of the organism. Then it collects (absorbs) it. Finally, when it contracts, it distributes the newly energized, oxygen-filled blood back out to the periphery, revitalizing the entire body.

New scientific devices to measure polarities of various substances and living things have been developed in Europe. These instruments, together with fifteen years of German research, reveal the startling fact that our environments alter and disturb our normal polarization and bioenergy and disrupt our nervous and glandular systems.

That bioenergy can be distorted or blocked is not a new theory, and this fact has been demonstrated with elementary physics. What is new is that many scientists and health researchers believe that life is steered or guided by specific frequencies and wavelengths of energy from the sun, cosmic background radiation, and the earth's magnetic field as they penetrate the nervous systems of animals and humans. Scientists realize now that natural sunlight contains a "necessary steering frequency" that can be adapted by the glandular systems only through the eye. Plants, for example, do not grow well under normal glass (which prevents certain "growth frequencies" from passing through), so special nursery glass is used to allow these steering frequencies to reach the plants.

The human nervous system is still a great mystery, yet this steering mechanism goes far in explaining why changes in the magnetic fields of the earth, moon, and sun cause changes in weather, crop and animal growth, and even human behavior. This steering phenomenon of "background radiations" can also help explain how swallows find their way to Capistrano each year from thousands of miles away—without benefit of maps or radar.

At the dawn of civilization, building materials, household items, and clothing were made only of natural substances and fibers. Housing was designed in an open, less dense format, using clay, wood, bricks, straw, earth, stone, and fibers. Man was more in resonance and in harmony with nature, and his housing, both in form and structure, permitted normal light as well as atmospheric and cosmic radiation to pulsate unimpeded through and around its inhabitants.

Gradually, as civilization progressed, more and more man-made and laboratory-fabricated materials and forms were devised that increasingly blocked man's biological and natural interaction with his pulsating, polarized surroundings. Humans slowly lost their intimate connection and "grounding" with the earth and their outdoor environment through the ever-increasing usage of man-made chemical, synthetic, and depolarized building materials in their home and work facilities.

It was in Germany that scientific environmental research proved that our typical modern buildings, electrical appliances, and lighting and electronic installations depolarize and seriously stress our nervous system, in turn disrupting normal hormone production. Ill health, increased stress, psychological problems, and sexual dysfunctions are the unhappy results of our ignorance of the "energy effects" that our buildings and technology have on the humans living and working in and around them.

Our bodies are inundated daily with all kinds of radiation from the atmosphere, indoors and out. The rate and amount of absorption depend on the sources from which the radiation emanates and how well (or poorly) one is screened in a controlled environment designed to use the beneficial forms of natural radiation (e.g., sunlight), rather than to be blocked by artificial, dense, sandwiched building material and technical installations.

Research reveals that certain materials found in homes and offices disturb the assimilation of bioenergy and its proper distribution in the body. Scientific instruments have been developed to measure the immediate hormonal changes in the blood when the human subject is exposed to "interference" by artificial electromagnetism or radiation from man-made materials and electronic devices.

Artificial building materials cause certain frequencies to be blocked from entering our dwellings and cause others to be doubled or tripled. German scientists found that these distortions effect an immediate change in the level of hormones in the blood (measured *in vivo*). Extensive experiments using thirty to forty commonly used building materials consistently produced an immediate effect—alteration in the nerve and hormonal response. Only natural materials such as untreated wood, brick, natural tile, and special glass, combined in a certain manner, allow the natural radiation to pass undisturbed into the body.

Many man-made building materials and electronic and electric installations, by blocking these signals, create a deficiency of necessary frequencies (information). Outdoors, microwaves and other man-made and -transmitted electronic radio emissions cause an excess of unnecessary frequencies to which our nervous system is unable to adapt. The result of this excessive stimulation is an electromagnetic exposure so strong that it overpowers the body's own subtle electrical energy. This effects an imbalance in the normal polarization of the body, reducing normal pulsations and causing stress, tension, and disease.

Research results have led to the construction of homes, offices, factories, and hotels with natural, bioenergetic building materials; development of shielding devices for electric circuits, appliances, and electronic equipment; and the use of lighting that is shielded and whose spectral effects closely match that of the sun itself.

In environments renovated or constructed with these bioenergetic methods, greater health and well-being are reported by the occupants. Deeper rest and shorter sleep periods are common, since the body stays polarized and is energized in a properly balanced and shielded indoor environment. Materials and insulations have been developed that let in the normal background radiations but essentially prevent many of the harmful forms from entering.

Those interested in more detailed information in regard to research and developments in bioenergetics may contact: Walter R.G. Kumpe, President, C.B.B., Inc., P.O. Box 31, Palm Beach, Florida 33480. Telephone: 305-832-3529.

EIGHT

Color for Exteriors

It appears that color on exteriors is currently having a renaissance. Chromatic environments that would have been unthinkable a few years ago are now being created. The attitudes and design philosophies conditioned to avoid the conscious use of color in the external city environment are, perhaps, on the decline. Leading architects are introducing color back into the environment, and fortunately this is beginning to change the face of architecture.

Good examples of this change, however, are still the exception rather than the rule. Analysis of recent projects and interviews with numerous architects, conducted by the authors, lead to the conclusion that many architectural firms still place emphasis on the achromatic, plastic qualities of their designs without attaching the same degree of importance to color. The principal architects of established and successful firms may well have difficulty in breaking with an education based to a great extent on the Bauhaus tradition. Younger architects working in such firms do not yet have sufficient seniority for effective implementation of their often more liberal ideas.

It is also true that most architects do not have the luxury or the freedom to design as they truly wish to do. Those much-publicized projects that serve as outstanding examples of the rebirth of color usually are the work of internationally known architects of considerable professional reputation.

The average architect often must compromise to satisfy the demands of his client. Developers of office buildings, mass housing, shopping centers, and the like, often are concerned with public reaction and therefore the salability of their projects. This leads to preconceived notions of public taste without a real understanding of people's desires and needs. Often local government officials also hold cautious views. Color might be mistaken for luxury by a taxpaying community; hence, public institutions such as schools and other government buildings appear the same, year after year. In both cases, there is a real danger of run-of-the-mill color choices.

It is to architects reluctant to consider color as an integral part of the total design process, and to the "willing" architect who needs help in educating reluctant clients, that this chapter is directed. External color not only is important in the psychological realm (archromatic versus chromatic), but also is an important element in the form of an architectonic ensemble.

THE PUBLIC'S ATTITUDE

People are very conscious of color and texture in the built environment, and they *do* like variations. The capacity to find enjoyment in looking at or living in the purity and severity of colorless, unadorned, or raw concrete buildings is limited to those who have the same aesthetic values as the architects of those environments. The general public usually associates such buildings with prisons or bunkers, and finds them cold, lifeless, and boring. Studies point out that the presence of color on exteriors gives rise to positive evaluations, while the absence of color is generally considered negative.

For many years, Sweden has taken an active interest in the study of people's reactions toward and evaluations of exterior environmental color. The Department of Psychology of the University of Göteborg conducted a series of investigations, and overall results show that the majority of people are critical of a lack of color and positive about happier colors. As L. Sivik summarized:

> From the interview questions, common to many of our investigations carried out in relation to the urban environment, it can be concluded that *people consider it self-evident that color is an important factor in*

environmental design [italics in original]. People also think that one is made happier by "happy" environmental colours and sad by dull environmental colours (Sivik, quoted in Porter and Mikellides 1976, 138).

In one of these investigations, 600 people were interviewed in two different housing areas—one with gray buildings and the other with strongly colored buildings. Those living in the gray area described their homes as "concrete boxes," "bunkers," and the like, while almost all of those living in the colored area were happy to have color in their environment.

Studies on people's attitudes toward external color are not confined to the Swedes. Oscar Newman, a New York architect, had the responsibility of modifying the grounds and facades of a low-income housing project built of gray cement block. Because of heat loss and weather penetration, the Housing Authority had decided to cover the block with three coats of cement. Newman took it a step further and "used this as an opportunity to go beyond this basic functional requirement and add both color and texture to the surface of the buildings and the grounds of the project." Residents coordinated proposed color combinations with their neighbors; restrictions on some colors were relaxed because residents reacted negatively to some of the more conservative combinations.

The project was a successful experiment in determining whether people would respond to external changes made to their living environment. In the first year and subsequent years, residents made their own extensive improvements to grounds and to the insides of their houses. It seems that the renovation had instilled a sense of neighborhood pride. Subsequent interviews showed that the changes to the building facades were valued more highly than the new lighting, benching, and fencing that had been provided.

Newman was criticized by the architectural profession for his use of color. Many felt that instead of elevating the taste of his clients, he had catered to their "low level" of taste. Perhaps color played only a cosmetic role (aesthetically), but Newman had the courage to satisfy a social need. It is doubtful that subjecting the residents to another visually boring environment would have raised their level of taste.

The drabness of colorless and austere environments has little in common with the creation of the inviting, psychologically healthy, and beneficial milieus in which people prefer to live. It is no surprise that many monochromatic environments experience vandalism and graffiti. Is it the residents' expression of displeasure? That certainly seems to be a possible answer. No one needs much training in psychology to understand that if an environment provides pleasure, it is not vandalized by those profiting directly from it. And the reverse holds true, of course, for the disliked environment.

Does the colorless environment germinate or contribute to some of our social ills? It seems to be a factor. Many teenagers with behavioral problems and drug addiction have mentioned in interviews that they "hated" where they lived or grew up. High-density complexes austere in architecture and color, small (if any) playgrounds, a shrub or patch of grass here and there—such are the environments that reflect impersonality and a disregard for human emotions. Obviously, one cannot be so naive as to forget that other factors, such as family interaction and economic considerations, are involved. Yet the environment is a contributing factor, one that builders and architects must heed adequately.

One of our own investigations provides a final example of how people react to exterior color. In Southern California, many housing complexes, shopping centers, and office buildings are being built in an imitation mission style of architecture. The predominant colors are white or off-white for walls and red or terra-cotta for roofs. We were interested in finding out whether the public had a great affection for the coloration, and, if so, whether it was based on association with tradition, and then whether this attitude could be changed by presenting alternatives to the white.

We produced color renderings of several existing housing complexes. We interviewed people living within those complexes and asked them how they liked the existing coloration of their buildings. It was not surprising to find out that most residents had never given much thought to the color, having considered it an integral part of the architectural style. The repetition of white over the years had instilled the belief that it had to be so. Interestingly enough, residents of complexes with an austere architectural form not reminiscent of the mission style hated the white coloration, calling it monotonous and boring.

After posing the first question, we presented the color renderings and asked: How do you compare your apartment complex with the one in color as shown in these renderings? Most residents were not averse to breaking with "tradition" and found a different coloration much more interesting, inviting, and pleasurable. (It should be mentioned that we did not replace white with another single color but with a variety of basic wall colors and stronger chromatic accents without losing the overall architectural unity.) Most people felt especially positive about having their unit be somewhat different from that of their neighbors. This might be due to a desire for a little individuality among residents of high-density housing.

Developers and architects we interviewed argued that the mission style is the cultural or historical heritage of the region—since it once belonged to Mexico. Yet Mexico is not unfamiliar with color in its architecture (nor is Spain). In speaking of California's tradition, it is not necessary to take the historical palette of missions as the only criterion. The totality of color used in its history (such as in marketplaces) should be used to convey a historical mood or evoke a sense of location.

Another argument is that of climate. It is evident that there is a relationship between color and temperature, since light and heat are both derived from the sun. White reflects light and therefore heat. Yet, if temperature control is the argument in Southern California's climate, then it seems odd that so many projects (aside from the mission style) are in earth tones, which absorb more heat than the colors we had proposed.

These studies and others seem to indicate that people prefer chromatic external environments over austere, colorless surroundings. Of course, what an architect considers pleasant does not always coincide with what the public likes. It is obvious that architecture cannot be relegated to mass consensus, but surely there must be a way to satisfy both the public's needs and preferences and the architect's aesthetic aspirations.

THE HISTORICAL MISCONCEPTION

To understand how the lack of color in exteriors evolved, it is necessary to review briefly some of the history of color in architecture, starting with Greek architecture.

Many scholars had thought that early Greek architecture used little applied color. Yet the appearances of ancient Greek environments were quite different from those historical sets illustrated in

Hollywood films. A white-marbled ancient Greece (and imperial Rome) is a misconception. Most buildings were painted in symbolic and sometimes cosmetic coloring. Some statues wore lipstick and false eyelashes. Ancient Greeks believed that the natural colors of wood, marble, bronze, and ivory were no substitute for the creation of the city as a total artform. Architecture, therefore, was covered with colored washes.

The Romans adopted the Greeks' use of environmental color. Their buildings were colored through the use of bright paints, gold, bronze, marble, and mosaic. Being practical, Romans left their sculpture unpainted (unlike that of the Greeks). Excavations at Pompeii uncovered a wide range of colors that in some cases were brighter and clearer than those of the Greeks.

The influence of the Roman Empire extended over almost all of western Europe, and, later, medieval architectural forms were covered with color. The coloring of medieval churches often was much brighter on the exterior than the interior. During this period, rich color was applied to the interiors and exteriors of important buildings. The cathedral of Notre-Dame in Paris had bright red, green, orange, yellow-ochre, black, and white on moldings and sculpture. There is evidence that the majority of similar buildings of the thirteenth, fourteenth, and fifteenth centuries in France also were decorated in color.

During the Renaissance and afterward, color moved into the interior. Artificial color on exteriors was abandoned in favor of natural colors. Since color was used spontaneously during the Middle Ages, it must have been of great importance and a reflection of the time and spirit. After that, the use of exterior color declined, especially during the Reformation, when color was considered sensuous, sacrilegious, and vulgar.

To understand "lack of color," it is necessary to return to the misconception that the Greek classical style of architecture was unpainted. The ravages of time eroded the rich environmental colors and exposed the natural surfaces of the building materials. Historians and architects accepted this as the coloring of ancient buildings. The Greek classical style has served as an inspiration to architects through the ages. Buildings in modern cities include Greek architectural elements—but without the colors that embellished the originals. The Parthenon has been considered the epitome of architectural perfection; it stands as a source of study in monochromatic excellence and purity, when in fact it originally was painted and detailed in rich color. These established misconceptions about the past have thoroughly conditioned attitudes and design philosophies against the use of color on the exteriors of our city environments.

Modern times have seen movements and countermovements in the use of color in architecture. One that had a great impact was that of the Bauhaus, a revolutionary and functionally sound school founded in 1919 by Walter Gropius. The Bauhaus established new modes of building design and construction, but with a definite lack of color and ornamentation. Gropius became the leading advocate of a purist and functionalist approach to architecture. White, clear, and bright meant freedom and space.

It seems odd that principles of color and color psychology were introduced into the teaching program at the Bauhaus. In the fine arts, such Bauhaus painters as Paul Klee, Josef Albers, and Johannes Itten produced some excellent work in color. Yet no allowance was made for it in architecture. The brave attack against the separation of art and architecture (a split that dates back to the Renaissance) succumbed to intrigues between the art and technology factions of the staff. Hitler's arrival on the scene and his subsequent 1933 purge of elements who opposed him resulted in the demise of the Bauhaus and also of the reunification attempts between art and architecture. America welcomed Walter Gropius, Marcel Breuer, Herbert Bayer, and Mies van der Rohe; the result was a radical change in architecture.

Architects who are graduates of Ivy League schools appear to have been educated in the Bauhaus tradition. Emphasis has been (and still is) on the linear representation of spatial dimensions. Perspective, plans, elevations, and projection drawings are the traditional methods of communicating architectural perceptions. Graphics are drawn or rendered in black and white, three-dimensional cardboard models are gray, and the whole emphasis is on the achromatic plastic qualities. The spatial effects that color can achieve and the fact that forms first reach the eye via color are often not understood.

BLEND IN OR STAND OUT?

Should architecture fit into the environment or stand out from it? Of course there are two schools of thought on this. Frank Lloyd Wright believed that architecture should blend into the environment, and therefore he utilized only natural materials. Colorful natural stone was as far as he would go; he rejected the use of paint and denounced color as the concern of the "interior desecrators."

Jean-Philippe Lenclos of France also works with the natural color palette; unlike Wright, however, he makes dramatic use of natural colors. In his early pioneer work, he endeavored to endow the built landscape with richly colored space that represented a painterly approach embodied in the philosophies of Fernand Léger and Victor Vasarely. Lenclos's color programs for gigantic machinery are widely known.

Lenclos creates his natural-color palettes by collecting regional color samples of natural earths and clays and incorporating the colors of vegetation, sky, and water. He always draws the samples from specific regions and then uses them in that region, making the results look appropriate and harmonious. This technique is more suited to rural and suburban regions than to crowded urban areas with a lack of vegetation.

Le Corbusier used color in architecture with less regard to natural environmental conditions. He had a great fondness for color and believed it can create a feeling of space. His compositions were based on sound geometry; in a Berlin apartment project, for example, he used red, yellow, green, and blue in a way that complemented the geometric architectural composition of the building.

Vasarely has revived the idea of the polychromatic built environment of ancient civilization, as Léger and the de Stijl movement tried before him. His is a new way, however, guided by the spirit of mathematics and modern science. He has broken out of the limitations of the artist's traditional role and redirected his use of color and geometric patterns toward the urban situation. His idea of the future role of artists is that they be reunited with architecture. His highest goal is the advancement of the polychromatic environment and an end to ugly cities. It is no more difficult to build something beautiful than something ugly. For gray concrete he offers polychromy, something that is not out of the question with modern technology.

Each architectural project must be evaluated from many different standpoints. However, it would seem logical that in high-density housing complexes and cityscapes with scarcely a tree, color could bring some needed relief or compensation. It is difficult to disregard two facts:

1. Research has shown that people are negative and critical of austere, colorless environments in our cities.
2. Color has psychotherapeutic effects that can be utilized to meet the psychological needs of people living in unresponsive, crowded environments.

Even the worst tenements can be improved by the introduction of color, giving some pleasure to those who live there. In this sense, the job is not only an aesthetic one but also a moral one. Old, drab, and derelict environments can receive a new face; newer gray or monochromatic urban surroundings can become "humanized."

Does all this mean that color can be applied at random, that, as long as it is strong and bright, all will suddenly be well? Of course not. Characterization and harmony through color can be achieved only with a great amount of professional experience; otherwise, it will never be truly outstanding. Color should be a consideration and an integral part of architectural planning from the onset, not a separate element that the architect has to deal with later for better or for worse. Otto Haesler once said:

> Advocating color in architecture involves much more than wishing to see buildings painted bright hues or wanting to improve people's taste in general. The task is a much larger one. It means taking the architectural value of each building and of entire streets and squares and raising it to a new level, increasing the overall effect. This job requires a lot of responsibility, yet by the same token it is extremely important that it be done.

Architecture must not be colored for color's sake. Color is a property and the language of form, not a separate element or an intruder. Color in environments need not forsake elegance if it is used intelligently and tactfully; as a matter of fact, it can lend an aesthetic quality that would otherwise be unobtainable.

NINE

Offices and Computer Workstations

The next six chapters offer detailed information on the use of color, and they also discuss other important design considerations for office, school, health-care, foodservice, and industrial environments. Color descriptions include such terms as pale yellow, light green, pumpkin, and beige, and although such identification is not exact, it does evoke mental images of color familiar to most people. More exact references appear in the Color Specification Tables. These tables, using Munsell and Glidden color notations, list some examples of the single colors and combinations specified in the text (for dominant colors only).

The color collages in this book are designed to help give visual impressions of color for specific spaces. Each color shown is also identified by its Glidden notation (some colors may change slightly during the printing process). Both the tables and the collages are examples and should not be considered the only correct color possibilities. There are countless workable uses of color that remain within the authors' suggested guidelines.

To begin with offices, it is important to recognize that business managers often overlook that employee efficiency and the work environment have a direct relationship. Worker-effectiveness studies have tended to concentrate more on industrial surroundings than on offices. This is understandable, because it is easier to measure the number of items coming off a production line than to establish and measure standards in office work.

Before the subject of specific colors, the three primary concerns in office situations should be: (1) strict adherence to the rules for safeguarding vision (outlined in chapter 5, with more details in the chapters that follow this one); (2) awareness of health risks from the biological effects of light on office workers effectively sealed off from natural light during daylight hours; and (3) awareness of the role of psychology. To this end, a few observations are relevant:

1. Drab offices are counterproductive. Off-white, buff, and gray surroundings offer little inspiration. Employers must reflect an image of caring for their employees, and this involves providing environments that will raise spirits, not suppress them.
2. Satisfaction with the environment is closely associated with job performance.
3. Office workers spend half of their waking hours on the job. A pleasant setting will positively reinforce their efforts to represent the company's interests.
4. Orderly environments inspire orderliness; chaotic surroundings may breed chaotic thinking.
5. Creating beneficial environments may have to go beyond visual experiences. Multisensory experiences may be introduced. This might involve moving from grand-scale public areas to personal-scale work areas, including a texture such as a rough stone wall in an incidental area.

Those businessmen who are worried about dollars and cents must realize that no matter what the cost of an agreeable office environment, it is still a fraction of the cost of developing and keeping employees.

We have no intention of creating the impression that humanizing the work environment means developing recreational or living areas. The objective should be to eliminate influences that interfere with tasks, be they visual, physiological, or psychological. Office workers are supposed to get things done, not be entertained. The design criteria must be based on objective and not subjective guidelines.

Unfortunately, many new corporate office buildings are so concerned about corporate image that a style or fashion approach is superseding good, practical sense. Often, too great an effort is made to create a design image that is associated mentally with the product or service the business sells.

Very popular, and fairly recent, is the "high tech" image. Heavy emphasis is placed on sterility or neutrality created by grays, white, and black, with an occasional dark hue (usually purple) in upholstery. One case history involves an office suite with white walls, black desks, and deep-purple carpets. Since white reflects 80 percent of light and black about 5 percent, the brightness contrast ratio is 16 to 1; this is outrageous.

One of the instances where gray is acceptable is on a desk top. A warm gray (about 30 percent) is ideal for working surfaces. The color is neutral and nondistracting, and it strikes a good brightness balance between white and black, keeping the eye at a uniform and comfortable level of adjustment.

Most offices today have adopted the so-called open-office system. The idea behind them is better communication—no endless corridors to travel and doors to open (no windows, either). This leaves little chance for the personal arrangement of one's own space (such as paintings on the walls or standing plants). It is also contrary to the long-held view that people work best within their own four walls.

The introduction of small, movable cubicles has minimized this lack of privacy somewhat. Colors for these can be used effectively to create an office "landscape." But one vision problem does arise— no allowance is made for the distant seeing required to relax the eyes.

On the subject of color specifications, first come the colors that should not be used: purple, violet, vivid yellows or yellow-green, bright red, and dark brown (except wood). And, please, no white or gray. Beyond that, the choice of hues, guided by good judgment, is fairly broad. It should be remembered that in offices where a great deal of concentration is required, attention should be directed inward with cool hues. In general office areas, the choice of warm or cool hues depends on preference; the use of such colors as soft yellow, sandstone, pale gold, pale orange, pale green, and olive tones is appropriate.

One side of a corridor might be beige, the other light orange, with an accent wall at the end in a medium tone of blue. Endwalls in offices are also worth considering. For color suggestions, see the office specification illustration in Appendix A.

THE VISUAL DISPLAY TERMINAL OFFICE—A SPECIAL CASE

It was estimated in 1984 that there were more than seven million workers in North America using visual display terminals (VDTs) (Macaulay and Pliniussen 1984). With the massive introduction of desk-top computers into offices, schools, hotel reservation centers, airlines, travel agencies, and so forth, undoubtedly this number is increasing daily.

Despite the advantages offered by such equipment, operators of VDTs have been the largest single source of health complaints registered with the National Institute of Occupational Safety and Health. According to a survey conducted by the Data Entry Management Association, more than 66 percent of the respondents reported they had experienced eyestrain, back pain, fatigue, and neck and shoulder pains. More than 33 percent had felt burning eyes and general irritability. Headaches and loss of visual acuity were also common complaints.

All too often, these grievances are blamed directly on the visual display terminal. Perhaps fault can be found with some of the more poorly designed equipment, but the VDT should not be looked upon as the foremost and only culprit. Desk-top computers are being bought and installed without adequate attention paid to lighting, glare, office layout, furniture, and the workings of the human optical system.

In most offices, work is scrutinized and manipulated on a flat horizontal plane. Illumination falls adequately and comfortably from overhead. Office tasks such as reading, writing, typing, and filing are done with the worker's line of sight directed primarily downward. Work on the VDT, because of the terminal screen's upright or near-upright position, requires the worker to raise his line of sight higher than he would if he were working on a horizontal surface.

In this position, there are mirror images of overhead lighting fixtures, off-white walls that veil the screens, and bright clothing that reflects into the eyes. In numerous cases, the room's illumination level is too high, causing a decrease in display contrast, which in turn reduces the legibility of the characters displayed on the screen.

Solutions have been suggested from studies that already have been made (more are on the way), but they must be implemented— and quickly. We have found surprising uniformity in most aspects

Potential sources of glare.

of the recommendations made in various American and European publications. It seems evident that adherence to these suggestions will substantially eliminate visual, physical, and psychological problems associated with VDT use.

The welfare of the VDT operator should be the primary concern of the employer. (No employer would contradict this statement.) However, there is another fairly obvious point to consider: Better environmental conditions increase efficiency, hence productivity. A 1984 study by the National Institute of Occupational Safety and Health showed that data-entry workers using ergonomically designed terminals were significantly more productive than others. The American Productivity Center revealed that improved furniture design can increase productivity by some 12 percent (Thachenkary and Harris 1984). The United States Department of Health and Human Services tested workers in the worst- and best-designed environments, and found that productivity increased by nearly 25 percent at some of the best-designed workstations (Barr 1984).

What follows is a detailed discussion of the causes of health complaints, and recommendations for correcting them by creating a beneficial VDT environment.

General Illumination Level

There is some controversy in regard to appropriate light levels for VDT workplaces. An excellent paper (1982) by William Cushman of Eastman Kodak reported that, at one extreme, the Swedish National Board of Occupational Safety and Health recommends 200 to 300 lux (19 to 28 footcandles). At the other extreme, the Canadian Defense and Civil Institute of Environmental Medicine recommends 75 to 100 footcandles (810 to 1075 lux). According to their 1981 *Lighting Handbook*, the Illuminating Engineering Society of North America recommends 5 to 10 footcandles (55 to 100 lux).

Cushman himself suggests 15 to 35 footcandles (160 to 380 lux) for tasks not involving paper documents, with a bit more light—35 to 50 footcandles (380 to 540 lux)—for tasks involving transfer of information from paper documents to VDT. There are others whose recommendations fall within the general scope of Cushman's specifications, thus tending to confirm these illumination values. To quote from the 1984 technical report *Human Factors of Workstations with Visual Displays*, published by IBM: "An average light level of about 400 lux (or slightly less) is usually satisfactory for office environments." (Four hundred lux is approximately 38 footcandles.) The pamphlet *Vision and the VDT Operator*, from the American Optometric Association, advises 30 to 50 footcandles (323 to 540 lux). A 1983 publication distributed by a German governmental agency (Bayerisches Staatsministerium für Arbeit und Sozialordnung) specifies 300 to 500 lux (28 to 46 footcandles).

There is no question that light levels in VDT workstations should be lower than those in general offices. It would be wholly appropriate to let workers decide efficiency and comfort levels for themselves by equipping illumination in computer rooms with dimmers. Three case histories conducted by Faber Birren illustrate the point that operators will, in all probability, choose illumination levels within Cushman's suggested range.

Workers in a New York office with computer-aided design equipment (paper documents were not generally involved) were free to adjust the available light level, which did not exceed 50 footcandles (540 lux). The operators selected a level of 20 to 24 footcandles (215 to 258 lux).

In the second example, an office's existing light level of about 85 footcandles (915 lux) was reduced to about 40 footcandles (430 lux) after the installation of new louvered fixtures controlled with dimmers. Complaints of eye fatigue virtually ceased. The VDT work in this office involved paper documents.

The third case involved a control room with an array of electronic equipment, including computers, in a paper mill. The situation was somewhat unusual. The facility, operated round the clock, required workers to leave the control room occasionally during the day to perform outdoor tasks. Since the iris of the eye constricts rapidly to brightness and adjusts more slowly to darkness, workers found, upon reentering the control room, that a light level of 100 footcandles (1076 lux) was necessary to allow them to see the computer screens clearly. This was due to a time delay in visibility. At night, however, the level selected was 40 to 50 footcandles (430 to 538 lux), because no extreme eye adjustments were required.

Close Distance and Frequent Eye Movements

By far, most health complaints experienced by VDT operators are associated with the eyes and vision. The nature of the work sets a high demand on the visual perception process. As stated earlier, human eyes are most efficient when looking at distances. VDT use, on the other hand, calls for intense scrutiny at close distance.

Long periods of concentration on the screen at such close range often causes visual fatigue. The external muscles (oculomotor) of the eye work together to keep both eyes centered on the same character and then to allow them to move from one character or word to another. Internal muscles—in this case, the ring of ciliary muscles—contract to compress the lens of the eye. This steady effort, as with any static muscle exertion, may cause the eye's muscular system to tire.

Optical relaxation is achieved by looking into the distance occasionally. Hence, there must be allowance for distance seeing of at least fifteen feet (4.6 meters). This pertains not only to VDT operators, but to all office workers who have their vision confined to near distance. The eye muscles must have a chance to relax.

Work involving reference material requires the eyes to shift among the material, the keyboard, and the screen—frequent changes in seeing from horizontal to vertical and back. Each time, the eye must change its focus (accommodate). This may also prove tiring, and it will be aggravated further if there is a large difference in luminous density among the reference material, the keyboard, and the screen. The American Optometric Society, along with others, suggests placing the reference material as close as possible to the screen to avoid great eye and head movements, and at the same distance from the eyes as the VDT screen—thereby also avoiding frequent changes in focus.

Controlling Glare and Brightness Contrast

Glare and extreme differences in light and dark cause a great amount of discomfort. Undue stress on the tiny muscles (iris) that control the amount of light entering the eye causes visual discomfort, headaches, nausea, general fatigue, and true pain.

It is essential to avoid at all costs reflected glare or specular images on the VDT screen from the operator's own bright clothing, light walls, or other objects above or behind the VDT. These reflections make it difficult to see the characters on the screen, because the display contrast is reduced, and some characters may be partially or totally obscured. In addition to the health risks mentioned in the preceding paragraph, neck and back pains may

Reflective glare on VDT screen (courtesy of Faber Birren).

result from attempts by the operator to read obscured characters or
to minimize glare by contorting posture.

How can glare be reduced or eliminated? The first consideration is the direction of lighting. Most offices have direct lighting
systems with overhead troffer fixtures and plastic lenses. These
should be modified or changed. If it is not possible to remove the
fixtures, it is best to replace them with better luminaires located so
they do not cause glare. In some instances, fixture lenses can be
replaced with louvered parabolic "egg crates." Lighting can remain
directed from above, but neither lamps nor images will be reflected
on the screen.

Light levels must be kept on the low side. Indirect lighting
from special fixtures may also be considered, or lights can be
attached to partitions or other stationary objects. Care must be taken
so that an illuminated ceiling does not create a veil over the VDT
screens.

In some instances, such as rented office space, changes in
lighting systems may not be allowed. The alternative is to relocate
the VDT equipment so that light sources do not reflect on the
screen. It would be ideal if VDTs were positioned so that viewing
direction, windows, and row of luminaires are parallel—i.e., there
should be no windows or luminaires directly behind or in front of
the operator. To clarify further, workstations must be placed between the rows of overhead light fixtures and not underneath them.

If these suggestions fail to eliminate glare, then other possibilities are circular polarizers, micromesh filters and louvered film,
and antireflection coating or etching. However, there are disadvan-
tages connected with antiglare filters. Depending on the type used,
there may be reduction in clarity of image, restricted viewing
angles imposing postural constraints, a need for frequent cleaning,
and high cost.

The control of brightness differences in the environment has
already been discussed, but it has important applications in VDT
offices.

Extreme contrast in light and dark must be controlled in all
areas: equipment, furniture, walls, and floors. Vision must be kept
at a uniform level by midtones, with no dark or light extremes. The
ideal ratio is 3 to 1, meaning that optimum visual comfort is
maintained when task luminance is not greater than three times the
luminance in the areas adjacent to the task. Walls in computer
rooms should reflect 50 to 60 percent. The figures are 20 to 30

percent for floors and 30 to 50 percent for furniture. The ratio for the low 20 percent and the high 60 percent would be 3 to 1.

Shades, venetian blinds, or opaque drapes should be installed on windows to block out excess daylight. If daylight cannot be blocked out completely, the row of luminaires parallel to the windows should be fitted with dimmers. Then, during the day, illumination levels can be lowered to compensate for the entering daylight; at night, they can be raised, since some light will be lost through the window.

Walls must have a matte or flat finish—never, never semigloss or gloss paint. It is important to respect the reflection ratios for walls (this rules out white and off-white walls). Within the ratios mentioned, color is optional. Attention is focused on the screen and light levels are low, so the color specifications for general offices given at the beginning of this chapter do not always apply. The VDT office is a special case. Some interest or change of pace may be added by the use of a different colored endwall.

The German color consultant Heinrich Frieling has suggested color specifications that compensate for the green characters of the VDT screen. He advises that the bothersome light-purplish-pink afterimages created may be intercepted by purple-brownish (grayed) coloration on the walls (green phosphor has a dominant wavelength of approximately 500 nm; the color was calculated from that). The color of the workstation should be olive-gray, which will gray the afterimage. Interestingly enough, some time ago the *Chicago Tribune* mentioned the color distortion VDT operators can suffer. In the wake of VDT safety studies, operators reported noticing pink edges on white paper and walls after prolonged periods of VDT use.

Computer Design, Equipment, and Furniture

There are several factors to be considered in the design of VDT equipment. The ideal equipment allows the operator to adjust the brightness of the characters and the contrast between image and background, and it has a screen that is separate from the keyboard to allow adjustment of the viewing distance. Individual characters on the screen as well as the text should be legible with the least amount of effort. Legibility depends on the size, contrast, clearness, and regularity of the luminous density of the letters, numbers, and symbols.

Brightness controls allow adjustment of the flicker effect (an increase in brightness increases flickering). Light emitted by the phosphors on the inside surface of the screen fades and must be refreshed. With a refresh rate of 60 hertz, flickering will not be detected by most operators.

Well-designed equipment calls for the ability to raise, lower, swivel, or tilt the terminal. Operators must have some control in positioning their equipment to suit their needs.

West Germany has developed a number of standards pertaining to workstation design, lighting, character shapes and sizes, sight lines, and viewing angles. What makes these standards effective is that unless they are followed by employers, the government may decide to make employers, not government, liable to pay any workmen's compensation cases that may ensue. The German specifications are respected throughout Europe, and they are making their way to the United States. If they are adopted here, many existing computer colors and brightness ratios will have to be revised.

For one thing, black keys would be out. Black is negative in its stimulation of retinal nerves. Particularly under relatively dim illumination, it is difficult to locate and see black. It may be argued that the proficient worker locates keys from memory, but the black area of the keys can be objectionable if a worker must alternately look at white paper beside the computer.

Except for use as letters, numerals, or symbols, white also is not recommended. West German standards for reflectances are: between 15 and 75 percent for computer housing (with 20 to 50 percent recommended); 20 to 50 percent for keyboard casing; 40 to 60 percent for the majority of keys; 15 to 75 percent for function keys. White has a reflectance of 80 percent or more, and therefore is ruled out. Keys should have a dull or matte finish to avoid specular reflections and highlights. Their color should be neutral, except for function keys, which may be colored.

A data (copy) holder should be available at those workstations where operators perform data entry from paper documents. The data holder should be adapted to the size of the documents and be adjustable in slope and height. As is the case with all equipment, its finish should be dull.

Office furniture must be conducive to the health and comfort of the worker. Backaches, neck muscle strain, and headaches can be attributed to bad posture. Chairs should be of ergonomic design and adjustable in height—not only to conform to different body sizes but also to enable the operator to sit at a proper angle to the screen. The top of the screen should be under eye height; the appropriate distance from eye to screen is approximately fourteen to twenty inches (thirty-five to fifty centimeters).

Machine stands or tables must be adjustable in height and sturdy enough to prevent vibration. The work surface must be large enough so that reference material can be placed favorably for reach and visual range.

What the VDT Operator Can Do

It is important that the VDT operator have periodic eye examinations by an ophthalmologist or optometrist. The eye specialist should know that the patient is a VDT operator, and it is wise to supply details about the workplace (viewing distances, viewing angles for screens). Sunglasses are inappropriate in VDT workstations.

Task Breaks

VDT work is demanding in all aspects, and operators should have more frequent breaks from their task than is usual for general office workers. A general rule is fifteen minutes every two hours for moderate VDT users, and fifteen minutes every hour for heavy users. This will allow relaxation of the eye and body muscles that have been held in a relatively fixed position for a long period. A static body position decreases the blood supply to muscles, resulting in premature fatigue.

T E N

Schools

School administrators and facility planners are faced with a dilemma. The taxpaying community demands an increase in efficiency and quality of their schools and simultaneously wishes to cut costs. Unfortunately, this often directly affects the choice of color used in the schools. For budget reasons, professional counsel rarely is sought, leaving the interior color planning to the notions of administrators, teachers, or the maintenance department. The last-mentioned are most concerned with ease of maintenance—the less color, the better—and the administrators and teachers choose color on a subjective basis, not on scientific principles. All too often, this results either in bleak environments or in the use of color for the sake of color—which accomplishes little that is constructive.

Educational leaders must recognize that the school's physical environment is a vital psychophysiological factor in study situations. Appropriate colors are important in protecting eyesight, creating surroundings that are conducive to study, and promoting physical and mental health. Many cases of nervousness, irritability, lack of interest, and behavioral problems can be attributed directly to incorrect environmental conditions involving poorly planned light and color. Studies have shown that a functionally and thoughtfully planned school interior facilitates learning new subject matter and improves scholastic performance.

VISION

It should be quite obvious that causes of visual discomfort (eyestrain and fatigue) have great bearing on scholastic performance. Once there is ample light to see clearly, attention must be given to control of glare and brightness. Principles that ensure comfortable conditions for vision have been discussed in previous chapters, and they must be followed strictly in school situations.

PRESCHOOL AND ELEMENTARY GRADES

Children of kindergarten and elementary-school ages are mostly extroverted by nature. A warm, bright color scheme complements this tendency, thereby reducing tension, nervousness, and anxiety. Good colors are light salmon, soft warm yellow, pale yellow-orange, coral, and peach. A kindergarten room could have light salmon as the dominant color on walls, with a moss-green floor and olive-green tables.

UPPER-GRADE AND SECONDARY-SCHOOL CLASSROOMS

Softer surroundings created by subtle and/or cooler hues have a centripetal action, which enhances the ability to concentrate. Beige, pale or light green, and blue-green are appropriate, and they permit better concentration by providing a passive effect.

In classrooms where students face one direction, it is particularly useful to make the front wall a different color from the side and back walls. The purpose of this is to relax the students' eyes when they look up from their tasks, thus providing effective contrast with chalkboards, materials displayed, training aids, and the instructor, as well as drawing attention to the front of the room. By adding interest to the classroom through a different appearance from different directions, visual monotony is avoided. Side and back walls may be in beige, sandstone, or light tan, while the front wall might be in medium tones of gold, terra-cotta, green, or blue.

LIBRARIES

Pale or light green creates a passive effect that enhances concentration in the library environment.

DOMESTIC ARTS AND MANUAL TRAINING

Luminous hues, such as light yellow and light orange, are appropriate for domestic arts classrooms, and beige or tan is suitable for manual-training workshops. Different-colored front walls are worth introducing.

GYMNASIUMS

In large areas, hues of high reflectance (such as found in light yellow) are preferable.

AUDITORIUMS

Light gold or salmon can create the warm atmosphere desirable in an auditorium.

CORRIDORS

More tolerance exists in these areas. The color scheme should be attractive and give the school a distinctive personality. In the lower grades (preschool and elementary), hues may be lively; in a multistoried school, each corridor can be treated differently. Complementary color schemes are quite appropriate. Good examples are light-orange corridors offset with blue doors, or light-green walls with red doors (not, however, reminiscent of fire doors).

ADMINISTRATIVE OFFICES

For these, follow the guidelines given in chapter 9.

LIGHT

In view of the research conducted on the biological effects of artificial illumination, serious consideration must be given to the use of full-spectrum lighting in schools. Sufficient evidence exists to warrant a strong recommendation of artificial sunlight, at least in classrooms, libraries, and gymnasiums, if not in all areas of the school facility (corridors may be excepted, if only for budgetary reasons).

To support our contention, we suggest a review of the publications discussed in chapter 6. Many of the sources cover the effects of artificial lighting on schoolchildren.

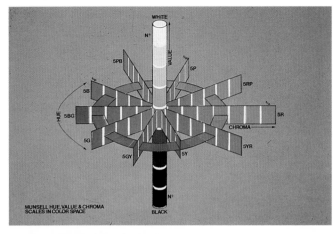

Munsell hue, value, and chroma scales in color space (courtesy of Munsell Color).

High-density apartment complex, Geneva, Switzerland.

High-density apartment complex, Geneva, Switzerland.

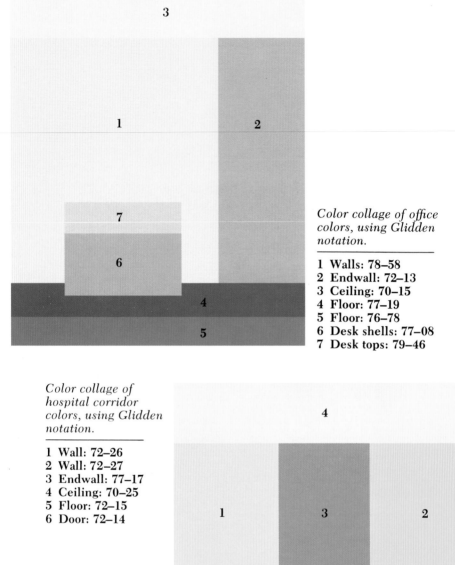

Color collage of office colors, using Glidden notation.

1 Walls: 78–58
2 Endwall: 72–13
3 Ceiling: 70–15
4 Floor: 77–19
5 Floor: 76–78
6 Desk shells: 77–08
7 Desk tops: 79–46

Color collage of hospital corridor colors, using Glidden notation.

1 Wall: 72–26
2 Wall: 72–27
3 Endwall: 77–17
4 Ceiling: 70–25
5 Floor: 72–15
6 Door: 72–14

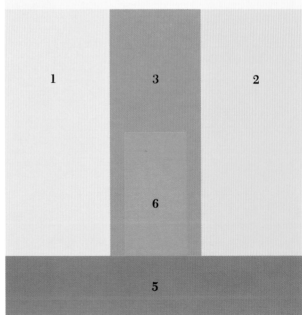

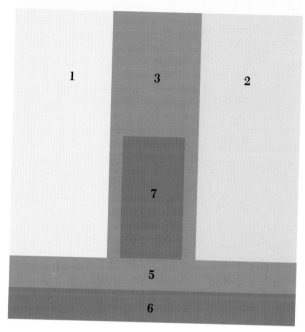

Color collage of
hospital corridor
colors, using Glidden
notation.

1 Wall: 72–98
2 Wall: 75–54
3 Endwall: 72–06
4 Ceiling: 70–12
5 Floor: 72–06
6 Floor: 76–07
7 Door: 76–07

Color collage of
hospital corridor
colors, using Glidden
notation.

1 Walls: 72–82
2 Ceiling: 74–98
3 Floor: 75–59
4 Door: 75–24
5 Door frame: 74–98

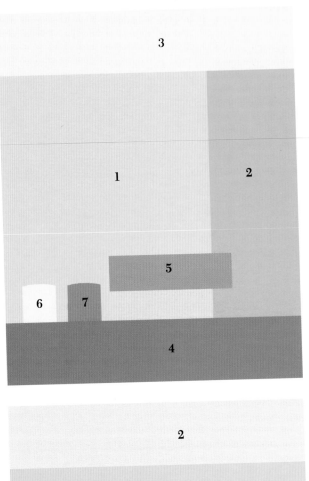

Color collage of
preschool colors,
using Glidden
notation.

1 Walls: 71–95
2 Endwall: 71–97
3 Ceiling: 72–49
4 Floor: 76–39
5 Table tops: 76–06
6 Chairs: 72–49
7 Chairs: 71–91

Color collage of
hospital patient
(maternity) room
colors, using Glidden
notation.

1 Walls: 71–72
2 Ceiling: 75–45
3 Floor: 75–59
4 Frieze: 73–62

Color collage of hospital patient (postoperative, long-term)
room colors, using Glidden notation.

1 Walls: 72–25
2 Ceiling: 77–05
3 Floor: 72–22
4 Nightstand surface,
   bedspread, uphol-
   stery: 76–77

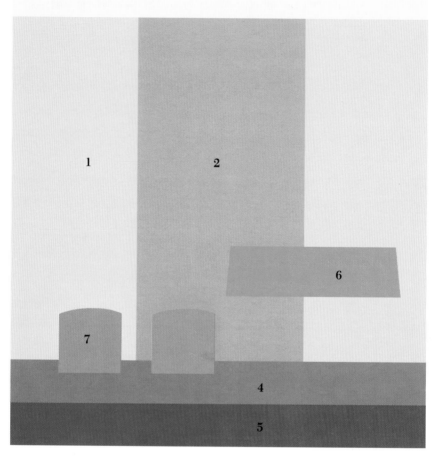

Color collage of hospital patient room, warm colors, using Glidden notation.

1 Walls: **72–26**
2 Endwall: **72–29**
3 Ceiling: **70–15**
4 Floor: **72–15**
5 Floor: **77–19**
6 Bedspread: **72–30**
7 Upholstery: **77–17**

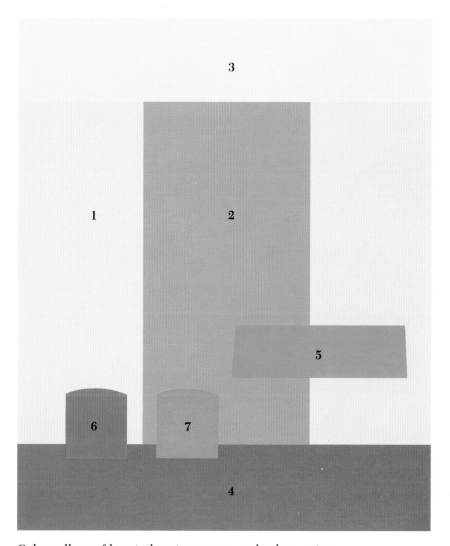

Color collage of hospital patient room, cool colors, using
Glidden notation.

1 **Walls: 72–58**
2 **Endwall: 75–57**
3 **Ceiling: 70–26**
4 **Floor: 72–15**
5 **Bedspread: 72–14**
6 **Upholstery: 76–06**
7 **Upholstery: 72–14**

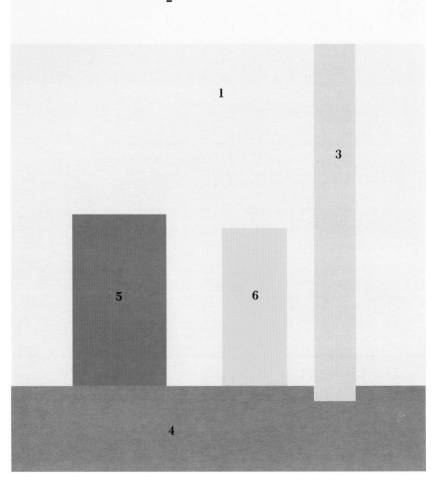

Collage of colors for industry (exposure to warm temperatures), using Glidden notation.

1 Walls: 76–34
2 Ceiling: 74–41
3 Columns: 76–36
4 Floor: 79–50
5 Doors: 72–15
6 Incidental areas:
  72–60

ELEVEN

Medical Facilities

Medical facilities have the highest priority in the application of a correct color environment, since the value of color as a psychother-apeutic aid has been recognized. Psychosomatic medicine has verified the strong ties that exist between the physical response to surgical and medical care and the mental and emotional attitude of the patient. A correct color environment contributes to the welfare of the patient and the efficiency and competence of the staff.

The best of medical care and nursing attention is demanded in hospitals. Patients and visitors are, therefore, critical and apprehen-sive. The interior appearance should not be so coldly formal as to seem aloof and unfriendly. The ill person needs to feel that he is being cared for—not just medically, but emotionally as well. On the other hand, a too-casual look might stimulate skepticism regarding the professional services. A hospital can retain a dignified and respectful appearance yet be attractive at the same time.

For that part of the medical facility where surgeons, nurses, and medical staff perform their duties (i.e., operating rooms, inten-sive care, X-ray, therapy, laboratories), the environment created cannot tax vision, lead to undue fatigue, or induce emotional mo-notony.

Hospitals deal with a broad cross-section of humanity, and it is wise to seek common denominators rather than to base color choice on personal preference or current interior-design idioms.

DEVELOPMENT OF A COLOR PLAN

1. In existing facilities, make a visual survey and preliminary notes to help in identifying environmental problems, lighting conditions, high-traffic areas, and other relevant information. Spend enough time in each section of the facility to get an impression of its heart, soul, and character.

    For newly planned institutions, a prerequisite is an understanding of the architectural drawings and proposed lighting. It must be kept in mind that light and color work hand in hand.
2. Verify and become familiar with the functions of each area in the facility (surgical, intensive care, maternity, long-term or short-term patient areas). Find out how long the space will be occupied by various people and what their activities are during that time. Collect enough data and impressions to be thoroughly familiar with the project.
3. Discuss the design objectives with the client.
4. Compile all data into three major categories: *Atmosphere*—patient rooms, corridors, lobbies, lounges, general office areas; *Task sections*—X-ray, therapy, examining, treatment, surgical, intensive care, work areas; *Functional areas*—utility, equipment, storage areas.

The foregoing information should provide an excellent basis for commencing color selection. The selection itself now depends on setting the correct environment for each of the categories by careful consideration of the psychophysiological effects and the technical aspects of color.

CORRIDORS

The mood or atmosphere of a ward depends on the colors used in the corridor. Whether this mood should be warm or cool depends in some cases on the function of the ward itself. For maternity and pediatric wards, warm colors are a good choice; for intensive care or recovery, we suggest cool colors.

In any case, the corridors should be attractive and reflect an atmosphere of calm. Calm, of course, does not depend solely on the use of cool color; the effect can be transmitted just as well by warm hues. Chroma, value, pattern, and amount of hue variation are the principles in establishing either an exciting or a calming effect. For example, a pale orange or peach will appear calmer than a bright, intense green.

With large areas, such as corridors, a common mistake is choosing color and pattern for an empty space. Let us assume a hypothetical situation. A designer is asked to design a hospital corridor. Since not much can be done in terms of accessories, a logical step would be to add interest with imaginative decorative effects in the form of designs or patterns on the walls, or maybe different-colored wall sections running horizontally in attention-producing hues. More interest comes from pattern in the carpet or a carryover of the wall designs to the carpet.

This plan certainly would have impact and be aesthetically pleasing when the proposal is presented. But now let us add people to that corridor—nurses busily going about their tasks, carts and equipment being pulled from one area to another, unsteady patients trying to navigate a path. The once-empty corridor on the presentation board abounds in pattern, activity, and visual information rate. Will this be a calm setting to reduce anxiety?

On the other hand, the designer could lessen the information rate by keeping the walls neutral, with color added in incidental areas. The absence of color creates emotional sterility and may not be calming (or attractive).

For a warm, cheerful effect, major walls can be light orange, orange-yellow, yellow; also beige (only with the two-color effect) and pale green. For instance: a pale yellow-orange for walls, moss-green floor, very light green ceiling, and pale green doors.

In long corridors, the two-color effect may be combined with a darker or complementary color at the end of the hallway. An example would be a peach on one wall of the corridor, a variation of that hue on the other side, and a dark tone of medium blue on the wall at the end of the corridor (endwall). For a more subtle and cooler effect, a light beige may be chosen for one wall, a pale green for the other, and a medium tone of red-orange for the endwall.

Brightness ratios should be similar for the two hues on the sides of the corridor. This will minimize contrast and establish a uniform field of view. There should never be one dark side and one light side. The color of the floor, and the side of the door that faces the corridor, should be either related to the dominant hue or complementary. Under no circumstances should there be too many radically different colors in the major areas of the corridor.

PATIENT ROOMS

To accommodate the temperaments of both introverts and extroverts, we make it standard practice to create alternating cool and warm patient rooms. Intensive care is the only exception to this rule. To be cool, rooms need not be depressing or uninviting—a concern often expressed among design students.

A good practice is to use endwall treatments in patient rooms, preferably on the wall the patient faces. One color, of course, predominates, with the endwall being a harmonizing hue. A cool room, for example, might have sandstone on three walls and pale green on the endwall. A warm room could be pale orange on three sides, with the fourth wall slightly darker but not brighter. If a single color is used for all four walls, suitable choices are rose, peach, soft yellow, pale gold, and light green. Because patients so often are supine, ceilings may also be tinted. The ceiling here may be the same color as the endwall, but much lighter—at least 50 percent white should be added.

For reasons of refinement, and the fact that strong colors may be unduly unsettling or grow monotonous to a patient confined for a long term, it is essential to exercise caution in purity of color. One major consideration is that the reflection of highly saturated hues on the patient may alter his or her skin color; this is hardly desirable in regard to visual diagnosis. Fairly soft tones are better than sharp ones. A long-term patient room (also postoperative for minor surgery) could have all walls in pale orange, the floor in dark red-orange, and the ceiling tinted in light blue.

The designer must exercise good judgment and some psychological insight. There is good reason to consider comfort of vision as a primary concern, as has already been pointed out, but psychological factors are also of great importance. Rooms should be suited to their function or type of patient—long-term, chronic, intensive care, postoperative, short-term, pediatric, maternity, and so forth. For instance, maternity rooms, to keep in the spirit of the anticipated happy event, could have walls in pink, ceiling in light green, and floor in moss green. Since cool colors are more conducive to relaxation, chronic patients should feel more at ease in light green or aqua. It would be illogical to reverse the surroundings for these two types of patients.

Never create a total ward environment in only warm or only cool hues (this applies to all areas of a health facility). One atmosphere may predominate, depending on the ward in question, but always introduce hues of the opposite color temperature somewhere.

INTENSIVE CARE

Reduced light levels are usual in intensive-care units. These areas need a restful and psychologically cool atmosphere. Aqua and lower-chroma greens or blue-greens are appropriate.

OPERATING ROOMS

The medium tone of bluish-green (turquoise) is advised without qualification for operating rooms. It is already utilized for the textiles used for gowns, caps, masks, and covers in surgery. This color reduces glare under intense light, aids in maintaining visual acuity, and improves color discrimination by complementing the reddish tint of blood and tissue. Recovery rooms can be lighter blue-greens, pale green, or aqua.

NURSES' STATIONS

The nurses' station is a key location and should stand apart visually. Regardless of the adjacent wall color, the back area of the station should be orange, yellow, gold, or blue-green in a medium or deeper value and somewhat stronger chroma. (Yellow, of course, would be the exception to the use of a medium or deeper value, because in those values it will turn brownish.)

THERAPY ROOMS

For radiation and physical therapy, aqua is excellent. It is cool and clean, reduces muscular tension, and gives a pleasing glow to complexion. In occupational therapy, pale orange or yellow will create a cheerful atmosphere.

LABORATORIES

Areas such as these, including sterilizing rooms, can be in tan, pale green, gold, or aqua. Pearl gray is excellent where good color discrimination is necessary.

EXAMINATION AND TREATMENT ROOMS

Pale green or aqua would be appropriate for cardiac, cystoscopy, orthopedic, and urology clinics; pale coral or a peach tone may be used for dermatology, obstetrics, and gynecology. In examination rooms, it is important to remember that the color must not be so saturated as to interfere with visual diagnosis.

PEDIATRIC WARDS

Every effort should be made to create an appealing and colorful environment for children. Too often, adults have a tendency to make decisions based on their concepts of what a child needs, without regard for research in areas of child development and child psychology.

The use of color in pediatric wards or children's hospitals is an entire subject by itself. A good rule of thumb is to use warm hues, with cooler hues in incidental areas.

NURSERIES

The problem of general illumination for hospital nurseries has been of great concern to the authors. We focused considerable attention on the argument over whether or not general lighting can help prevent hyperbilirubinemia (infant jaundice). Studies on the treatment of infant jaundice gave short shrift to the topic of prevention. Some of the literature that did touch upon possible prevention seemed contradictory or vague at times in its recommendations. The issue was finally settled to our satisfaction by T.R.C. Sisson, professor of pediatrics and director of neonatal research at the Newark Beth Israel Medical Center. Dr. Sisson also alerted us to other concerns in nursery lighting that may well affect the health and welfare of infants.

For the moment, we will return to the issue of possible prevention of infant jaundice through general illumination. In hyperbilirubinemia, there is a high concentration of bilirubin in the blood. Bilirubin, formed from the hemoglobin of red blood cells during their normal breakdown, is excreted after undergoing chemical reactions in the liver. In the first days of life of an infant, especially a premature infant, the liver may not be fully functional in this respect. If high levels of bilirubin are allowed to persist, the result is kernicterus (brain staining), which leads to various degrees of mental and motor retardation, and even death. According to Thorington, Parascandola, and Cunningham(1971), the incidence of hyperbilirubinemia associated with prematurity is sufficiently widespread (about ten to twenty percent of prematures may be so afflicted) as to be of general concern.

In 1958, R. Cremer noted that infants placed near windows showed less jaundice than those located away from incoming natural light. This led to experiments with artificial light that showed bilirubinemia declines under the influence of visible blue light. To date, it has been found that the best spectral emission in the treatment of infant jaundice is 445 to 450 nm (blue light). A number of other studies have been made showing that energy in the green region and artificial full-spectrum light can also degrade bilirubin.

Since full-spectrum light simulates natural global radiation, it could be argued that this might be an effective general light source in the prevention of infant jaundice. Yet it does contain the UV element. Could that be damaging to skin and eyes? In a letter to the authors dated February 3, 1986, Dr. Sisson remarked:

> There is no doubt in my mind that general lighting which would add significant output in the UV-A spectrum can be hazardous. Although the cornea does not absorb UV-A, the lens does. It is not known how much UV the developing (i.e., neonatal) eye can safely absorb, nor what is a safe dermal exposure in such infants—safe enough that UV damage to the relatively thin skin of the newborn will not occur, or that the exposure (whose depth is increased above that of visible light because of the short wavelength) could not exceed the capacity of inherent cellular repair mechanisms.
>
> Reliance upon a general nursery light source of broad spectrum including UV-A to prevent hyperbilirubinemia would be misplaced: it would have little or no discernible effect in either prevention or treatment.

This, then, would indicate that the photic energies necessary to handle infant jaundice far exceed the environmental lighting of nurseries. In short, it is doubtful that general lighting, including full-spectrum light, is an aid in the prevention of hyperbilirubinemia.

In the latter part of 1985, the press reported on the hazards to vision from high levels of illumination in hospital nurseries. This was based on a study by Penny Glass and associates that appeared in *New England Journal of Medicine* in August of the same year. The study stated:

> In summary, this study suggests that the levels of light common in the hospital nursery may contribute to the incidence of oxygen-induced retinopathy of prematurity, especially in infants weighing less than 1000 g at birth.

To explain further, we quote Dr. Sisson from his editorial that appeared in the same issue of the journal:

> The impact on the newborn of the crisis atmosphere of the intensive care unit—its bustle, noise, and perhaps more important, its unremittingly brilliant illumination—has had scant regard compared with the attention paid to space requirements for the machinery of intensive care, visualization of monitors and skin color, pumps, tubing, access to the patients, and so on. The report by Glass and her associates in this issue of the *Journal* draws attention to this by showing a relation between the light environment imposed on newborns and the incidence of retinopathy. Glass et al. observed that the incidence of retinopathy of prematurity in two infant intensive care nurseries was greater among infants exposed to high illumination (60 ftc) [footcandles] than among infants kept under reduced lighting (25 ftc).

What recommendations can be made for nursery lighting? What will probably prove best is a general light source with minimal spectral deviation (high CRI), which will aid in visual diagnosis and in evaluating conditions of jaundice, cyanosis, and anemia, without the inclusion of the UV element. General illumination should be muted, but not to such an extent as to interfere with the procedures of care for the newborn or to cause visual deprivation. Local light sources can be installed to make it possible to see one infant without exposing others to high illumination levels at the time of observation.

The study by Glass et al. points out that some evidence indicates that cycled lighting may protect against damage caused by light. Constant or uninterrupted lighting is inappropriate, and, as

Dr. Sisson points out, "may disrupt fundamental physiologic and metabolic processes in the newborn." A workable solution may be to install dimmers that control each row of overhead luminaires separately. That way, nurses can control light levels and raise the levels as needed in particular areas. Philip Hughes, director of the Environmental Photobiology Section of the Duro-Test Corporation, has informed us that studies currently are looking at low-level illumination cycled with higher levels to simulate the dark/light cycle of night and day.

Specification of color in the hospital nursery should take into consideration visual diagnosis and observation. Pink or blue walls, which might delight parents, will not help nurses in their job of observation. Skin tones may be altered by yellow, pink, blue, green, and gray—a fact often overlooked by designers. A blue wall may make an infant look cyanotic (besides having the objections discussed in previous chapters); yellow or green walls may give a jaundiced look. With the exception of the ceiling, white should not be used. Reasons for this have also been amply discussed in this book. Light hues—weak in chroma and toward the neutral side (pale beige, sand)—are acceptable as long as adequate attention is paid to light-reflection ratios (not too high).

OFFICES

Where tasks demand a great deal of concentration, cooler colors should be used to direct attention inward. In general office areas, more freedom can be allowed. See chapter 9 for details.

LOBBIES AND RECEPTION AREAS

These areas usually convey the first impressions of the facility to the patient or visitor. The atmosphere should be friendly, yet dignified.

STAFF LOUNGES

Lounges should be different from other areas. Wallcoverings or textured patterns will help to create a personal atmosphere.

SANITARY FACILITIES

Reflection from coral or peach tones will cast a pinkish glow to enhance a patient's appearance.

CAFETERIAS

See chapter 13.

REJECTED COLORS

Certain colors that should be ruled out for hospitals are discussed below.

White, Off-White, and Gray

See chapters 2 and 3.

Yellow-Green

Avoid yellow-green, which tends to appear bilious and whose reflection on human flesh gives the complexion a sickly appearance. Specifications made in this chapter have included soft, pale yellows, and these should be toward the warmer side, because cool yellows may have a greenish look under fluorescent light with a low CRI rating.

Red

In practical situations, pure red seldom is used. Psychologically, the color is too aggressive and advancing. Mentally, it is associated with blood, and it is obvious why there are objections against its use in hospitals. Variations of pure red, such as rose, maroon, coral, and pink, are much more suitable.

Blue

Blue is appropriate in incidental areas and only then in a medium or deep tone. It has not been successful in medical facilities, because it tends to be cold and bleak if applied to large areas. Pale blue is sharply refracted by the lens of the eye and therefore tends to cast a haze over details and objects in the environment. This causes slight distress to some people who may be confined to an area for a long period. Blue-green is much more fitting.

Purple

Psychologically, purple may appear disconcerting and subduing. It is also associated with mourning, which would make it inappropriate in hospitals.

ART

Art should be a primary consideration in hospital decoration. It adds to the attractiveness of the surroundings and thereby furthers the image that the facility cares about the people it serves.

Special attention should be paid to pediatric wards, where art can be used as a form of communication. It can lessen anxiety and aid cognitive abilities and the perception of reality. But no flying elephants or crying clowns, please! A fantasy world will not aid the child, especially a younger one, in coping with the reality of having a problem treated while he is immersed in an environment he has difficulty understanding. The art that is selected should communicate a sense of caring, gentleness, and reassurance.

A NOTE ON FLOORING

Exercise caution in the selection of flooring, whether it be carpeting or vinyl composition tile (VCT). It is wiser to keep it simple and have a uniform field of view than to use too much pattern or different color design cut-ins. Refrain from highly polished pale floors, which produce glare and visual distortions by reflecting mirror images.

LIGHTING

In view of the research conducted on the biological implications of artificial light (see chapter 6), it seems obvious that hospitals should not use lighting that deviates considerably in its spectral composition from what is found in natural light.

In addition, fluorescent lamps that emit a balanced spectrum are particularly important for visual diagnosis. Unbalanced light sources are also unfavorable to the appearance of the patient. Visitors may find it difficult to give proper encouragement to the hospital patient if they show undue concern for the sickly appearance of skin tones. As has been mentioned, lighting with a slightly warm quality will enhance complexion better than the cool types. The Illuminating Engineering Society strongly recommends color-improved lights, such as the Deluxe lamps (those with a higher CRI rating), in health care facilities.

Artificial full-spectrum lights may also be used in many areas of the hospital (except the nursery), especially for patients who are required to be indoors for a long time.

T W E L V E

Mental Hospitals and Health Centers

The objective in mental hospitals and health centers is to eliminate their institutional appearance as much as possible. Staff members in mental hospitals and health centers ceased wearing uniforms long ago, and for good reasons. A less formal relationship exists between patients and staff. Barriers of mistrust and hostility are being broken. The uniform was a reminder of the institution and being institutionalized.

It seems that this philosophy should have been, or should now be, carried over into the patients' environment. Unfortunately, many of the facilities for the mentally ill are still drab, monotonous, and depressing. The mental health facility becomes a home for its patients—the average time spent there is longer than that spent in medical facilities. Therefore, the designer must create a climate that will decrease anxiety and suspicion and reflect an overall milieu of concern for the individuals undergoing treatment there. Treatment program and environment must complement each other.

The positive effects of correct environmental conditions can be quite dramatic. In 1978, we were asked to develop a color plan for a mental health center in Chula Vista, California, treating emotionally disturbed children and adolescents. This facility experienced a much greater amount of destruction than that produced by the normal exuberance of children and teenagers.

The facility was primarily recolored, using principles established by research into the psychophysiological effects of color. In each ward, an environment was created that would be beneficial and relevant to the particular age group of the occupants and the function that was expected of each area. Walls, furnishings, accessories, and flooring were color-coordinated.

The plan made use of a variety of colors. Most of these were pastel orange, yellows, peach, light green, turquoise, and blue (in incidental areas)—interspersed with rust and copper. In the children's corridor, yellow and orange contrasted with cooler colors on the doors and door frames. One side of the adolescent-unit corridor was tan, the other light green. Both colors were set off by tangerine, again, on doors and door frames. The adolescent patient rooms alternately had cool and warm tones so that the staff could try to assign introverted personality types to surroundings that suited them best. As one reporter wrote, "The net effect looks cozy but at the same time sophisticated."

Careful attention was given to the use of paintings and wall decorations. In the children's ward, themes reflected a reassuring quality, a sense of caring and gentleness. The philosophy was to establish a form of communication and aid cognitive abilities. The subject matter was not that of a fantasy world, but real situations with which a child can identify. In the adolescent units, the artwork ranged from impressionism and post-impressionism to contemporary styles of various types.

The remodeling started in early 1979, one unit at a time. As each unit was completed, the vandalism there diminished. By the conclusion of the project, the destruction had declined to almost nothing. The deliberate angry demolition of property simply had ended.

The project received a fair amount of press, radio, and television coverage. The magazine *Health Care Horizons* mentioned it under the headline "Health Center Finds Color Therapeutic." Indeed it did. As research clearly indicates, light, color, and sensory variety, when utilized intelligently, can go far as definite therapeutic and psychotherapeutic agents.

Skeptics began to suggest that the vandalism had subsided because a new and fresh environment had been created, and the occupants—remembering the old surroundings—were unwilling to live in an abused environment again. The contention was that any redecoration would have produced the same effect. However, that was not the case, since the facility had been redecorated before. If any new environment would have produced the same results, why did it fail to do so after the previous redecoration?

After almost six years, the facility is still being monitored. The patient population has changed many times over, and there has been no report of significant destructive behavior toward hospital property. Questionnaires produced one year after the completion of the new environment showed that, in addition to an immediate positive effect on patient behavior, staff morale also had increased. This surely speaks well for the use of color—utilized correctly and in conjunction with scientific guidelines.

Mental hospitals are highly dependent on the influence of the environment on the well-being and recovery of its patients. Light and color, in particular, may influence behavior and social interaction. Light and color must serve as psychological aids to recovery, or at the very least be instrumental in the development and maintenance of well-being.

The balance between unity and complexity is an extremely important design consideration for mental facilities. Patients housed in mental hospitals are prone to experience hallucinations. Their environment must not generate, or be supportive of, the continuation of hallucinations.

A monotonous environment, one that is low in stimulus, may well produce hallucinations. Sterile and uninteresting surroundings—deprived of sensory stimulation and offering few opportunities for human interaction—fail to stimulate conscious brain activity in the patient. In the absence of stimulation, the mind tends to seek some source, any source, of stimulus. Subsequently, it begins to seek greater meaning in the flow of thoughts and inner images. During the hallucinogenic process, the patient may get so locked up in his or her inner world that it becomes difficult to participate in what is considered reality.

On the other hand, too much information also will be supportive of hallucinations. Too many signals, or signals that conflict with one another, produce a kind of sensory chaos that the disassociating patient has difficulty sorting out, separating, and assigning to relevant categories. The manic and the schizophrenic have particular difficulty in filtering, selecting, and editing sensory experiences.

In their most vulnerable phases of illness, patients may find that rooms with strong colors overwhelm their sensory systems. The presence of strong color can bring forth associations or prod the patient to relive incidents. In some cases, the color stimulus may be carried over into other sensory channels, and the patient might experience synesthesia—hearing, feeling, or tasting colors.

Another circumstance that may present an opportunity for hallucination is that of visual deception. The environment should be perceptually honest, not deceptive. Mirror reflections of faces in glass partitions, glass doors, or other shiny surfaces may convince the patient he is "seeing things." There are countless such situations that the designer must learn to recognize and attempt to correct.

From a practical standpoint, it is difficult to tailor the patient's personal surroundings, such as his bedroom, to his particular mental disorder. The constant change in population is a considerable handicap. Yet, it is possible to follow an overall practical set of recommendations, listed below:

1. Color specifications for corridors, patient rooms, and examination rooms should follow the same general guidelines as those presented for medical facilities.

2. Recreation areas, lounges, and occupational therapy rooms should be in warm colors, such as orange, coral, or yellow. These colors will create an atmosphere conducive to the functions of these spaces.

3. Quiet or seclusion rooms should not look like punitive environments. If a patient has to be isolated, he or she should be in a cozy, inviting, and sparsely and safely furnished room. This does not mean that the room should be barren—just simple and uncluttered. The room should give the impression of refuge, protection, and recuperation—not punishment. Sensory overload should be avoided and relaxation furthered by cool colors such as greens or blue-greens. These must be chosen carefully so that they are soft and under no circumstances look "institutional."

4. For cafeterias and dining rooms, see chapter 13.

THIRTEEN

Food and Foodservice

Color plays a substantial, if not ultimate, role in our judgment of the freshness, ripeness, and palatability of food. Deviation from established associations and expectations seldom are accepted or tolerated. Sometimes the natural color of certain foods is rejected in favor what it is "expected" to be. Although people may have different preferences for certain colors of food, by and large there are common denominators.

The food industry is well aware of color conditioning, and processors treat food to retain natural color or apply food color where necessary. Packaging, too, plays an important role. Bread, cereal, and nuts are controlled precisely during baking or roasting so that they emerge neither too light nor too dark. Light beers are brewed pale yellow and often sold in green bottles, while strong beers are deep brown and sold in red or dark brown bottles. Dairy products, which consumers associate with coolness and hygiene, have blue or white packages. For butter packaging, gold or silver may indicate luxury; yellow and green might suggest the country-side. Some meat counters are illuminated with lights whose spectrum is closer to red, making the meat seem redder and more succulent.

Appetite depends on the sense of sight just as much as on smell.

Experiments have been done with people's appetites being stimulated by dishes containing the finest of delicacies shown under normal light. The substitution of colored light produced nausea. Dark-gray meat, orchid potatoes, muddy-violet salads, black peas, and blue bread found no takers—even though the people knew the food was edible.

Psychological studies on appetite appeal and color reveal a certain trend. Warm reds (vermilion, flamingo, coral), oranges (peach, pumpkin), warm yellows, light yellows, and clear greens are true appetite colors. Purple-violet, purplish-red, orange-yellow, yellow-green, mustard, grayed tones, and gray have little appeal. To be more specific, a peak of appetite and agreeable sensations exists in the red-orange and orange regions. Pleasure decreases at yellow-orange, increases again at yellow, reaches a low at yellow-green, and is restored at clear green. Blue-greens (aqua, turquoise), although seldom associated with food itself, are well regarded and can be used to advantage as backgrounds for food display.

A few observations are relevant here in regard to complementary colors and food, although they might not always be feasible from a practical standpoint. Green salad may look greener and fresher on cool pink serving dishes; the richness of butter is enhanced by green-blue or bluish-white; bread appears best on blue-green or green-blue plates.

Establishments where food is served or displayed could well profit from these findings. Personal whims in the choice of color can turn out to be quite unprofitable.

RESTAURANTS

No one factor makes or breaks a business, but a number of combined factors can do so. In the restaurant business, success rests on four conditions: food, service, price (usually at least a consideration for the average mortal), and ambience. As long as the criteria for good food and service (including decent price) are met, the inviting and attractive restaurant will always be the more successful one. People do not eat in restaurants solely to provide their bodies with necessary nutrients. They hope to spend an enjoyable hour or two in a "dining experience," and this certainly includes relaxing in an agreeable atmosphere. (Establishments catering to the "quick lunch" crowd are discussed later, for they, too, should delight the eye.)

Light is as important a factor as color in the design of an attractive restaurant. The first rule in providing a good lighting ambience is that it should be neither too bright nor too dark. Bright lights do not create cozy or intimate surroundings. Although one is aware in a restaurant that many others are present, it is essential that there be personal space to attain a desired degree of privacy.

Personal space comes from the placement of the tables, as well as through light, which should illuminate the table's surface well but not exceed that boundary. Local incandescent light is ideal, with other lighting (such as wall lamps and hanging lamps) strategically placed to illuminate entrances, exits, passages from kitchens, and any other areas needed to ensure safety. Bright overhead lighting destroys the feeling of personal space. It may be appropriate for places where mass social interaction is desirable, but it has no place in an intimate dining environment.

Nor should light be too skimpy, as with the ever-popular single candle in a glass container. Guests like to see their food (including its color), and they find it annoying to be faced with a dark mass on a plate. Also, trivial as it may seem, eye contact is an important part of social interaction and conversation—to which darkness does not contribute.

A restaurant's decor should take into account the hues that appeal to the appetite. In the red region, flamingo or coral is perfect; in the orange region, peach or pumpkin will provide a lively mood. It is wise to exercise caution, however, in regard to the color's saturation; if it is too pure, it can appear cheap and common. Accents may be darker reds, turquoise, or a medium tone of blue. Pale greens are also appropriate in certain instances, as are clear greens for accents.

Walls, tablecloths, dishes, furniture (if it is not natural wood), and upholstery should harmonize in analogous and complementary colors, and the unappetizing hues should be avoided. Complementary accents are appropriate—for example, blue-green carpets or tablecloths with flamingo walls. Among the high-appetite-appeal colors, there are enough possible combinations to satisfy the most discriminating soul. Psychological appeal, distinction, and a feeling of harmony and identity are always linked to products that sell well, and that also applies to foodservice establishments.

The following case history may illustrate one final point about restaurant design. A newly opened restaurant failed to attract the response that was envisioned. Although the restaurant owners wished to convey an atmosphere of exquisiteness and refinement, the choice of colors came from a misguided and ill-advised conception of elegance. Major walls were light gray, accented with shades of bluish-gray; tablecloths and upholstery were snow white. The result would have delighted a penguin, but it left customers cold. Elegance must not be perceived as aloofness; coldness and sterility are uninviting and certainly not relaxing. Gray is not an appetite color. People do not like gray meat, so why should they be expected to look at gray walls?

What is the point here? The same message we hope we have conveyed throughout this book: The intelligent use of color prevails over the intuitive one. Personal whim or fancy is arbitrary at best. Design trends come and go and there is nothing new under the sun. Studies have been and are being conducted by experienced personnel probing people's attitudes, reactions, and subjective feelings toward various environmental conditions, including foodservice establishments. These findings should be considered, followed, and respected. Restaurants are big business and competition is hard—even more of a reason to disregard personal interpretations of beauty in favor of a sound, practical approach.

CAFETERIAS AND COFFEE SHOPS

In formal restaurants, colors should be somewhat refined and subtle. Cafeterias and coffee shops, on the other hand, may be a bit brighter, although colors should not be intense or aggressive. Red-orange, orange, pale yellow, warm yellow, apricot, beige, and pale green are good as dominant wall colors (yellow should not be too bright) or for accents; blue and blue-green should be used only for accents.

Laminated tabletops may be in wood grain or the colors specified as appealing to the appetite. Because of its sterile appearance and for reasons of maintenance, white should not be used. For purposes of hygiene, floors should not be too dark. Texture or pattern may help to conceal nonremovable stains.

To ensure privacy, the serving line should always be separated physically from the people who are eating. If this is not possible, at least it should be done visually with dividers or large plants. Mahogany tables, reddish brick walls, wrought-iron grillwork, and vines around ceiling supports are great favorites in cafeterias.

Many businesses provide cafeterias, or break areas that often serve as lunchrooms, for their employees. The primary purpose in such areas is not just eating but also relaxation and recuperation. A total break from the work routine is necessary—for physical as well as mental reasons. Therefore, it is advisable to create surroundings that differ in light and color character from those found in the work environment.

The lighting milieu should be on the soft side, with hanging lamps (incandescent) low enough to illuminate only the table surface, and other local lighting at strategic places. Overhead fluorescent light is not always ideal in foodservice; if it must be used, the illumination level should be lower than is customary for work areas. Incandescent sources—such as standing, table, or wall lamps—may be added to low-level fluorescent illumination.

Warm light is imperative in all foodservice establishments. It flatters the complexion, creates coziness, and adds to the effect of warmth, thus inducing the desire to relax. The CRI of fluorescent light is important here, because we all eat with our eyes. Higher illumination levels are necesary at the service counter; they should never be of the cool-white variety if the dining area has incandescent or warm-white lighting. This juxtaposition will make the appearance of food and human complexion look especially unflattering.

FOOD DISPLAY

Food stores should follow the same color specifications that have been given so far—and avoid the unappetizing colors. Because of merchandise shelves, there is not much wall space available to apply color on, but some wall areas may be colored to make packaged items stand out, or to provide orientation through color association: clear green for produce; sea green for seafood; bright yellow for baked goods (an association with golden wheat fields and sunshine); pale yellow for dairy products (suggesting butter and cheeses); dark red-orange for coffee and chocolate (brown, unless it is wood, is not appropriate, especially as paint). It is important to make sure that the background colors do not interfere with the merchandise colors.

In the meat section, turquoise or sapphire blue on a background wall or fixtures will enhance the color of the meat. (The meat trays themselves should be white to suggest cleanliness.) Illumination must be warm and not cool white.

Fixtures for refrigerated items should be white or cool colors (such as light blue or aqua) to convey the feeling of coldness. Food items displayed in refrigerated units colored orange would look out of place.

On a final note, floors should be unobtrusive; all eyes should be directed toward the merchandise.

FOURTEEN

Industry

The tasks performed in various types of industries may be physically demanding, tedious, repetitive, and monotonous; expose workers to unusual levels of heat, noise, or odor; and place great demands on vision. As mentioned earlier, correct environmental conditions aid human efficiency and have a marked influence on worker morale and physical well-being—just as incorrect conditions will have a reverse effect. It is self-evident that this ultimately will affect the quality and quantity of production.

Previous chapters have contained fairly specific recommendations for use of color. Environmental recommendations can be made about such types of work as health care, education, and office work because, within each field, the work is performed in the same basic manner. Industry, on the other hand, is quite a different matter. Manufacturing businesses are as diverse as the products they produce. It would be simplistic to say that only one way is correct, and thereby cover all types of industries. Too much depends on knowledge of the nature of the work being performed, the character of materials or products produced, the kind of equipment used, and the dimensions of the plant area.

However, certain principles having to do with vision as well as functional uses of color and safety are common denominators for all industrial environments. Some basic guidelines are suggested below, including some general advice for various industries.

EYE FATIGUE

The tempo of modern production is much faster than ever before, requires greater accuracy and precision, and thus places an ever-increasing demand on the eyes. Although vision was discussed earlier, it should be emphasized again that the causes of visual fatigue and distress are the result of improper illumination (either too high or too low), glare, extreme changes from light to dark (brightness contrasts), and prolonged fixation of the eyes without suitable areas and distances for visual relaxation. The principles set forth in chapter 5, along with the additional guidelines that follow, should prove of benefit in minimizing eye fatigue.

1. Insufficient contrast between the work surface and the items being assembled or inspected may prove as uncomfortable as too much contrast. It is tiring to assemble a green object on a green work surface because of the extra effort required to differentiate between the two. A neutral (gray) work surface with about thirty percent reflectance would be best. In those instances where products being assembled are consistently the same color, the work surface should be the complementary of that color, but with proper reflectance and saturation (grayish). This also will aid in eliminating the menace of afterimage.
2. Background shields may also be used for delicate visual tasks. Such shields reflect light and provide contrast with materials, hold eye adjustments at a relatively stable level, confine vision to the task at hand, and cancel out background movement by providing a sense of isolation.
3. Work surfaces—and walls when possible—should have matte or dull surfaces to avoid reflected glare. For walls, there are paints that are durable and washable without being high-gloss.
4. If machines are positioned so that a wall is constantly in the immediate field of vision, it is important to control brightness contrast by establishing approximately the same brightness and using colors that rest the eyes. A dark wall and a light machine, or vice versa, demand unnecessary eye adjustments when vision is directed from the machine to the wall and back again.

5. Surfaces must be provided to rest the eyes, and such surfaces, if possible, should be similar in brightness to the work surface. These may be in pleasing tints with a reflectance of 25 to 40 percent.
6. In general, walls should reflect 50 to 60 percent if floor and equipment are dark, and 60 to 70 percent if most surfaces and areas are light. Machines, equipment, tables, and desks should have a reflectance ratio between 25 and 40 percent.
7. Walls containing windows must have a light color. Dark walls adjacent to sunlight shining through windows will result in unnecessary brightness contrasts.

COLOR CONSONANCE AND COMPENSATION

Color may support, conform, or be in agreement with a given situation; therefore it has a consonant action. When it counteracts specific environment problems, it may be said to have a compensatory action. For example, the problem of heat in an environment will be supported by a warm color such as orange and counteracted by the subjective coolness of blue-green. Orange has adopted the consonant role and blue-green the compensatory one.

Particularly in industrial surroundings, environmental conditions may become so bothersome as to be a real burden for the worker. In some industries (such as perfume and food processing), smells can be so penetrating that workers almost taste them. Irritating, repetitive noise from machines and equipment may be increased optically (see chapter 2) and become even more disturbing. These and other problems can be minimized by the compensatory action of color. This "color action" can serve as a measurement or guideline for the choice of a dominant color within the environment.

The colors listed below can supply action in either a consonant (increasing) or compensatory (decreasing) role for a variety of problems often encountered in industry. However, not all of them qualify for dominant wall colors; they may be used for incidental areas or machinery. The designation *maximum level* refers to those colors with which maximum consonant or complementary action is achieved, although other colors may work. Green, for instance, is conducive to the impression of coolness, but blue-green creates the impression to a greater extent.

Temperature

Heat is supported by red through orange and compensated for by blue, blue-green, light green, and white.

Cold is supported by green-blue and white (maximum level) and compensated for by red-orange, orange, and brown.

Noise

High-pitched sounds are supported by yellow and compensated for by olive green.

Muffled sounds are supported by dark colors and compensated for by light colors.

Smell

Sweet smells are supported by red and pink and compensated for by green and blue.

Narcotic and heavy smells are supported by brown-red and violet and compensated for by yellow-green and orange-yellow.

Bitter smells are supported by brown/violet and compensated for by orange/pink.

Sour smells are supported by yellow/yellow-green and compensated for by red/purple (maximum level).

Musky smells are supported by greenish-brown and compensated for by light blue.

Moisture/Dampness and Dryness

Moist or damp conditions are supported by green-blue (maximum level) and compensated for by yellow-tan (sand).

Dry conditions are supported by yellow-tan (sand) (maximum level) and compensated for by blue-green (maximum level).

Muscular Effort and Speed

Tasks involving a high degree of muscular effort and speed are supported by lively colors and compensated for by sedative and relaxing colors (see chapter 2).

MACHINERY

Machines and equipment are meant to serve man, and not vice versa. Therefore, they must have colors that serve the functional process by improving the perception of the critical or operating parts of the machine. Also, the machines need not be a separate or intruding element in the environmental visual presentation; they can be integrated so that they are part of an overall pleasing whole (safety permitting). Below are some considerations in the coloring of machines and equipment:

1. Focal colors (any color that commands attention through its brightness or contrast to surrounding colors) direct the eye to the critical or operating parts of a machine. Eyes are attracted to the brightest or the most contrasting area in the field of vision. Focal color on machinery discourages eye travel and also supports quick location of parts needed to operate the machine. For instance, a green machine may have light-beige working parts and red off-buttons or handles. Too many accents (no more than five), however, could create brightness contrasts.
2. Bases for machinery or equipment should be painted darker than the body color. This makes them appear steadier and more solid.
3. Gray machines demand a colored background.
4. There should be sufficient contrast between the machine and the material being fabricated to establish an easy-to-see line of division; otherwise, the operator is constantly straining to see where the material ends and the machine begins. For instance, blue-green would provide good contrast for brass fabrication; orange would not.
5. Large, numerous, and closely spaced machines should not be highly saturated or too dark in color. Too many objects in a space will add to complexity and present a spotty effect. Therefore, they should be colored so that they appear to recede (less saturated or lighter colors).

HEAVY INDUSTRY—LARGE-SCALE ASSEMBLY

General Guidelines

1. The ceiling should always be white or a very light color. This is essential to the efficiency of natural and artificial light.

2. Since work is often performed in large spaces, a rhythmic color arrangement on columns may produce variety.
3. Where noise is the prevailing character, compensation comes from the use of green tones as the dominant color. For subdominant surfaces, ochre may be introduced.
4. A lack of light in dark spaces may be compensated for by yellow.
5. Control tasks require full concentration. Disturbing visual background influences may be eliminated by screens.
6. The body color of cranes should be yellow, since yellow is highly visible and suggests caution.
7. Area divisions, important for retaining some order, are often designated by painted lines on the floor; these should be in yellow or white.

FOUNDRIES

General Guidelines

1. Compensation for heat must be made by the choice of blue-green or green/blue-green for all major surfaces, such as walls and equipment.
2. Light orange-yellow in incidental areas, such as columns and smaller wall areas, can offset the predominant blue-green on major surfaces.

WOOD PROCESSING

General Guidelines

1. The smell of wood generally is considered pleasant, and no compensation needs to be made.
2. Room colors may be green or olive tones (the natural look), with red-orange or orange accents. Avoid brown and tan or colors closely resembling that of wood itself, which would create a monotonous visual arrangement.
3. Warm light is more suitable than cold to enhance the inherent colors of wood.

LEATHER INDUSTRY

General Guidelines

1. The dominant color of the room should contrast with the color of the product.
2. The heavy odor of the leather may be compensated for by light, airy colors, such as light green or light yellow on major walls and light blue on incidental areas.
3. The color of the work surface for the leather-cutting process is important. For brownish leather, a light green work surface is ideal. A similar color contrast between work surface and leather should be maintained for leather dyed other colors. Leather dyed green, for example, should not be cut on a light green work surface.

CHEMICAL AND PHARMACEUTICAL INDUSTRIES

General Guidelines

1. The desired impression of hygiene and cleanliness must not lead to the use of white (usually the machines already are white). The same impression may be transmitted by using green or blue-green.
2. The dominant cool-colored atmosphere may be broken up by warm-colored (red-orange, orange) chairs, doors, and laboratory smocks.
3. A warm and stimulating atmosphere in corridors and break areas should be provided to give employees a change from the normally cool working atmosphere.
4. Where good color discrimination is necessary, work surfaces must be in neutral gray, as should background shields, screens, and walls (in the immediate area) to avoid color reflections.

BASIC SAFETY COLORS

1. *Red* is the basic color of identification for fire-protection equipment (exit signs, alarm boxes, extinguishers), containers holding dangerous contents, and buttons or switches on machinery.
2. *Orange* designates danger and is used for machine parts that may crush, cut, shock, or injure in some way. It is also used on

exposed edges (pulleys, gears, rollers, or other moving parts) and on starting buttons.

3. *Yellow* suggests caution and identifies physical hazards (obstructions, low beams, pillars, posts). Materials-handling equipment, cranes, and hoists are painted yellow.

4. *Green* is the basic color for safety. It is used to identify first-aid stations and kits.

5. *Blue* identifies electrical controls and special repair areas.

6. *White* is the housekeeping color used for the location of trash cans, trash receptacles, drinking fountains, and food-dispensing areas.

7. *Black-and-white striping* is standard for traffic areas, such as endwalls of corridors, and to indicate the locations of stairways and aisles.

PIPELINE IDENTIFICATION

It is essential to have proper identification for fluids and materials transported in pipelines. Although sometimes color codes are devised to suit individual operations (not all plants require the same breakdown), the following fundamentals will establish correct standards:

1. *Red* is used for fire-protection materials.

2. *Orange* identifies dangerous materials (steam, high pressures, caustics).

3. *Yellow* signals easily ignited and explosive materials (gas, acids).

4. *Green, white, gray, or black* indicates safe materials (water, air) that pose no hazard to life or property.

5. *Blue* identifies protective materials for purposes other than fire protection (gases that act as antidotes, foams).

FIFTEEN

A New Role and a Challenge

In his technological advancement, man often is accused of despoiling land, polluting air, contaminating water, and setting himself up in conflict with nature instead of acting in harmony with it. Organizations are formed worldwide to save the trees, animals, water, and everything else that is precious to us in nature, and that we depend on for survival. It is understandable to show concern and wonder where it will all end.

Who is to blame? Technology, industry, and progress, of course! Yet the average person is not likely to agree to give up the comforts modern technology has provided—nor can he, because most of them are now basic elements of his survival. It is difficult to imagine that modern man's idea of life in harmony with nature coincides with his living in a log cabin, growing and hunting his food, and traveling by oxcart because the automobile is a source of air pollution.

The solutions to environmental problems will be found not by regressing but by resorting to man's ingenuity and his technology. Already ways have been found to reduce industrial pollution, clean up waterways, and provide cleaner air. Technology has even come to the rescue of nature itself, performing such tasks as turning deserts into thriving food-producing areas.

From the time when man first moved into a cave to find shelter from the elements and built fires, he has progressively established himself in opposition to nature. Today he works, lives, and plays for the greater part of the day in artificial surroundings under his control—switching on lights, regulating temperature, and shutting out noise at will.

All efforts these days are directed toward the man-made environment. Rural areas are growing smaller, while urban centers continue to grow at a rapid pace. The dream of one's own plot of land under God's clear blue sky and the splendor of nature as far as the eye can see is fairly well removed from reality for the majority of people. Those fortunate enough to call themselves homeowners usually look out of the window not at distant fields but at someone else's backyard. Others live in apartments sandwiched between those of their neighbors.

In 1973, it was estimated that 75 percent of the United States population was urban, and this is a worldwide phenomenon, not just an American one. Most people in our industralized nations conduct their daily lives indoors or surrounded by environments of man's invention, and it is doubtful that this situation ever will reverse itself.

Architects are visualizing underground communities as well as above-ground cities enveloped in domes. Perhaps colonies one day will exist on our moon or on distant planets, and we will have to be totally independent of nature. Needless to say, more will be known by that time about our psychological and physiological functioning in relation to the three major components of the man-made environment: artificial light, color, and visual pattern.

Environment is a big challenge—not just for the future, but now. With modern technology and modern methods of analysis, research is uncovering heretofore-unknown evidence about these components. Interestingly enough, many early statements made by color pioneers—often disdained by designers as inconclusive or personal opinion—now have been substantiated.

As the human race is being propelled increasingly into the artificial environment, man is becoming more of an indoor species, along with all the consequent psychological and physiological effects. This situation demands a new role and new professional critiera for the designer.

Most interior architects or designers think of their profession as being more closely related to art than to science, but the time has come in which both must walk side by side. The members of the design community, whether they are architects (often involved in interior color choice), interior designers/decorators, color consultants, or lighting engineers, must think of themselves as being in the business of creating healthy environments to promote or safeguard physical and mental well-being.

If this is to be our goal, then we must recognize that interdisciplinary education is an absolute necessity. We often think that our aesthetic decisions—guided by a special intelligence or an innate gift—are more than sufficient for dealing with environmental problems. This just is not so. Familiarization with the psychological and physiological aspects of man–environment research will not limit our aesthetical expression or professional aspirations. On the contrary, it will enrich them.

Küller has correctly pointed out (1981) that there is a gap between research and practical application (including education). "It seems nobody is out there willing to listen," said one investigator in expressing his concern. The three-year research project conducted by our firm investigating this situation also substantiates the existing low correlation between research and application.

Yet, there is also reason for optimism. Symposia and conferences are being held worldwide to discuss color, architectural psychology, and the biological effects of light. Universities and even governments are initiating and supporting research related to man-made environments. There is also the International Association of Color Consultants (I.A.C.C.), an organization that has recognized the importance of an interdisciplinary approach. The group's work is discussed in Appendix B.

The job of creating the man-made habitat has never been as important and challenging as it is today. To the aesthetical dimension of their profession designers must now add the one having to do with human psychological and physiological reactions. If this challenge is accepted, the man-made environment and the profession creating it are headed for a brilliant future together.

Tables: Radiation Wavelengths/ Notations and Color Specifications

Table 1. Division of Radiation Wavelengths and Their Notations

Radiation	Notation	Wavelength (in nanometers)
Ultraviolet*	UV-A	315–400
	UV-B	280–315
	UV-C	100–280
also		
	Ozone-producing	180–220
	Bacterial (germicidal)	220–300
	Erythemal	280–320
	Blacklight	320–400
also		
	Far UV	100–200
	Middle UV	200–300
	Near UV	300–380
Visible	Violet	380–436
	Blue	436–495
	Green	495–566
	Yellow	566–589
	Orange	589–627
	Red	627–780
Infrared*	Near infrared	770–1,400
	Intermediate infrared	1,400–5,000
	Far infrared	5,000–1,000,000**

*Source: Lighting Handbook, the Illuminating Engineering Society, 1981.
**equals 1 millimeter.

Table 2. Color Specifications for Offices by Glidden Notation

General Offices		Corridors: Two-Wall Effect	
Walls:	72–26	Wall 1:	78–58
	72–51	Wall 2:	72–26 *or* 72–27
	72–59		
	73–23	Accent:	71–98 *or* 77–17
	75–54		
	76–35		
	78–59		

Private Offices with Endwall Treatments			
Walls:	78–50	*with*	Endwall: 76–37 *or* 77–17
	78–58	*with*	72–13 *or* 72–28 *or* 72–29
	72–74	*with*	72–28 *or* 77–08

Table 3. Color Specifications for Offices by Munsell Notation

General Offices		Corridors: Two-Wall Effect	
Walls:	5Y9/4	Wall 1:	10YR9/2
	10YR9/2	Wall 2:	7.5YR9/4
	7.5YR9/2		
	10YR9/4	Accent:	2.5YR7/8
	10YR8/2	*or*	2.5PB6/6
	10GY9/2		
	2.5BG9/2		

Private Offices with Endwall Treatments			
Walls:	10YR9/1	Endwall:	7.5R7/4
		or	5YR8/4
		or	5BG7/4
		or	7.5B6/6

Table 4. Color Specifications for Schools by Glidden Notation

For Concentration	Auditoriums	Gymnasium	Manual Training	Domestic Arts
Walls: 75–56	72–27	Walls: 78–23	78–66	72–12
76–35	72–59			

Cafeterias	Libraries	Restrooms	Classrooms with Accent (Front) Wall Treatments		
Walls: 71–65	72–76	75–56	Walls: 78–49	Accent:	72–06
72–05		77–64	or 78–66		72–78
72–12					74–63
72–36					76–06
					77–18

Table 5. Color Specifications for Schools by Munsell Notation

For Concentration	Auditoriums	Gymnasium	Manual Training	Domestic Arts
10GY9/2	10YR8/4	5Y9/4	10YR8/2	5YR8/4
2.5BG9/2	7.5YR8/6			

Cafeterias	Libraries	Restrooms	Classrooms with Accent (Front) Wall Treatments		
5YR8/4	2.5Y8/4	5G7/2	Walls: 10YR9/1	Accent:	7.5R6/4
10R8/4		5PB7/4	10YR8/2		10YR7/6
5R7/8					5G6/4
5YR7/8					7.5B6/6

Table 6. Color Specifications for Medical Facilities by Glidden Notation

Corridors: Two-Color Effect		Nurses' Station Back Wall	Chronic/ Intensive Care	Physical Therapy
Warm	*Cool*			
Wall 1: 72–26	78–49	Walls: 72–14	75–53	Walls: 76–35
Wall 2: 72–27	75–54	76–54	76–35	
Accent: 72–14	72–06			

Occupational Therapy	Examination and Treatment	Laboratories	Surgical/ Operating
72–26	Walls: 72–05	78–33	Walls: 76–38
	72–19	78–74	
	75–56	75–56	
	76–35		

Recovery	Patient Rooms	Patient Rooms with Endwall Treatments		
76–35	Walls: 72–05	Walls: 72–58	Endwall: 75–57	
	72–26	72–26	72–29	
	72–69			
	75–56			

Table 7. Color Specifications for Medical Facilities by Munsell Notation

Corridors: Two-Color Effect		Nurses' Station Back Wall	Chronic/ Intensive Care	Physical Therapy
Warm	*Cool*			
Wall 1: 7.5YR9/2	10YR9/1	Walls: 2.5YR6/10	10GY8.5/2	Walls: 2.5BG9/2
Wall 2: 7.5YR9/4	10G8/2	10BG6/6	2.5BG9/2	
Accent: 2.5YR7/4	10R7/6			

Occupational Therapy	Examination and Treatment	Laboratories	Surgical/ Operating
7.5YR8/4	Walls: 10R8/4	10YR9/1	Walls: 5BG6/4
	5YR8/4	10YR9/2	
	10GY8.5/2	5G7/2	
	2.5BG9/2		

Recovery	Patient Rooms	Patient Rooms with Endwall Treatments	
5BG7/4	Walls: 5R7/4	Walls: 10YR9/2	Endwall: 5Y8/6
2.5BG9/2	10YR8/4	10YR9/1	5G8/2
	5G7/2		
	5YR8/4		

Table 8. Color Specifications for Foodservice by Glidden Notation

Appetite Colors	Restaurants/Cafeterias/ Coffee Shops			Food Stores		Food Display (Meats)
71–95	Walls: 71–81	Accents: 76–37	Walls: 71–81	Offset by: 72–12	76–09	
72–12	72–36	77–17	72–05	72–45	76–38	
72–45	72–45			75–77		
73–23						
75–77						
71–81						

Table 9. Color Specifications for Foodservice by Munsell Notation

Appetite Colors	Restaurants/Cafeterias/ Coffee Shops			Food Stores			Food Display (Meats)
10R8/4	Walls: 5R7/8	Accents:	5BG7/4	Walls: 10R8/4	Offset by:	5YR8/4	2.5BG9/2
5YR8/4	5YR7/8		7.5B6/6	5R7/8		10GY9/2	5BG6/4
5Y9/4	5YR8/6					5YR7/8	
10GY9/2							
7.5R5/12							
5R7/8							
5YR7/8							
5Y9/6							

APPENDIX B

The International Association of Color Consultants

In 1957, with the participation of individuals from twelve countries sharing a mutual interest in the field of color, the International Association of Color Consultants (I.A.C.C.) was founded. The motivating force was an acute shortage of professional consultants, and an absence of possibilities for competent training in the field.

At first, in Holland and Belgium, the I.A.C.C. conducted courses that led to the title of Color Consultant. Since 1958, these courses, in the form of seminars, have been held in Salzburg, Austria, under the direction of Heinrich Frieling, president of the I.A.C.C. Docents from Sweden, Britain, West Germany, France, Belgium, the Netherlands, Switzerland, and other parts of the world instruct an increasing number of students from various countries in established knowledge of fields related to color and environment.

The Salzburg Seminars for Color and Environment are recognized for a comprehensive interdisciplinary approach to areas connected with color: physics, psychology, color psychology, physiology, biology, visual ergonomics, light technology, color systems, art, and so forth. Interdisciplinary training such as this is the most important prerequisite for a competent command of the laws of color. Therefore, the aim of the Salzburg seminars is not to train "specialists" who master only a limited professional area, but rather to shape professionals with comprehensive capabilities in all the areas of knowledge needed to create beneficial environments.

Not only can future color consultants study in Salzburg, but also those who, through the nature of their professions, come in contact with color problems: architects, designers, lighting engineers, psychologists, and so on. The total course consists of six seminars conducted in the spring and fall over a period of three years. Students gain practical experience from assigned exercises carried out during the months that the seminars are not in session. Completion of the total course, which includes a final examination before an international examining board, earns the student the title of "Color Consultant I.A.C.C. with diploma."

As of very recently, the I.A.C.C. is represented in the United States. The current aim is to present the interdisciplinary approach to color to the American design community, and to those organizations and associations concerned with color and environment. The ultimate goal is to provide an educational program similar to that in Salzburg. For further information about the I.A.C.C., contact the authors at 730 Pennsylvania Avenue, San Diego, California 92103.

Bibliography

Albers, Josef. *Interaction of Color.* New Haven: Yale University Press, 1963.

Ali, M.R. "Pattern of EEG Recovery under Photic Stimulation by Light of Different Colors." *Electroencephalography and Clinical Neurophysiology* 33 (1972): 332–35.

Arehart-Treichel, Joan. "School Lights and Problem Pupils." *Science News* 105 (April 1974): 258–59.

Asher, Harry. *Experiments in Seeing.* New York: Basic Books, Inc., 1961.

Barr, Danielle D. "Are Computer Screens an Office Menace?" *ABA Banking Journal* 76 (May 1984): 198, 202.

Beral, Valerie, et al. "Malignant Melanoma and Exposure to Fluorescent Lighting at Work." *The Lancet* (August 1982): 290–93.

Berlyne, D.E., and P. McDonnell. "Effects of Stimulus Complexity and Incongruity on Duration of EEG Desynchronization." *Electroencephalography and Clinical Neurophysiology* 18 (1965): 156–61.

Birren, Faber. *Color Psychology and Color Therapy.* New Hyde Park, N.Y.: University Books, 1961.

———. *Color for Interiors.* New York: Whitney Library of Design, 1963.

———. "Color It Color." *Progressive Architecture* (September 1967): 129–132.

———. "Color and Man-Made Environments: The Significance of Light." *A.I.A. Journal* (August 1972).

———. "Color and Man-Made Environments: Reactions of Body and Eye." *A.I.A. Journal* (September 1972).

———. "Color and Man-Made Environments: Reactions of Mind and Emotion." *A.I.A. Journal* (October 1972).

———. "A Colorful Environment for the Mentally Disturbed." *Art Psychotherapy* 1 (1973): 255–59.

———. "Light: What May Be Good for the Body is Not Necessarily Good for the Eye." *Lighting Design and Application* (July 1974): 41–43.

———. "The 'Off-White Epidemic': A Call for a Reconsideration of Color." *A.I.A. Journal* (July 1977).

———. *Color and Human Response.* New York: Van Nostrand Reinhold Co., 1978.

———. "Human Response to Color and Light." *Hospitals* (July 16, 1979): 93–96.

———. *Light, Color and Environment.* rev. ed. New York: Van Nostrand Reinhold Co., 1982.

———. "Color and Psychotherapy." *Interior Design* (December 1983): 166–69.

Bond, Fred. *Color: How to See and Use It.* San Francisco: Camera Craft Publishing Co., 1954.

Branley, Franklyn M. *Color: From Rainbows to Lasers.* New York: Thomas Y. Crowell Co., 1978.

Brody, Jane E. "Surprising Health Impact Discovered for Light." *New York Times,* November 13, 1984.

———. "Personal Health: Compensating for the Lack of Sunlight in Winter, Which Can Affect the Body and Emotions." *New York Times,* November 14, 1984.

Cheskin, Louis. *Colors: What They Can Do for You.* New York: Liveright Publishing Corp., 1947.

———. *How to Color-Tune Your Home.* New York: Quadrangle Books.

Chevreul, M. *The Principles of Harmony and Contrast of Colors.* 1839. Reprint edited and annotated by Faber Birren. New York: Reinhold Publishing Corp., 1967.

Clark, Linda A. *The Ancient Art of Color Therapy.* Old Greenwich, C.T.: Devin-Adair, Publishers, 1975.

Crewdson, Frederick M. *Color in Decoration and Design.* Wilmette, I.L.: Frederick J. Drake and Co., 1953.

Cushman, William H. "Lighting for Workplaces with Visual Display Terminals (VDTs)." Paper presented at the American Industrial Hygiene Association Symposium on Visual Display Terminals, Denver, Colorado, March 1982.

Dantsig, N.M., D.N. Lazarev, and M.V. Sokolov. "Ultra-Violet Installations of Beneficial Action." International Commission of Illumination, Publication C.I.E. No. 14A, Bureau Central de la Commission (1968): 225–31.

Düttman, Martina, Friedrich Schmuck, and Johannes Uhl. *Color in Townscape.* San Francisco: W.H. Freeman and Co., 1981.

Ellinger, Richard G. *Color Structure and Design.* New York: Van Nostrand Reinhold Co., 1963.

Eysenck, H.J. *Fact and Fiction in Psychology.* Harmondsworth, M.D.: Penguin Books Ltd., 1965.

Feller, R.P., et al. "Significant Effect of Environmental Lighting on Caries Incidence in the Cotton Rat." *Proceedings of the Society for Experimental Biology and Medicine* (1974): 1065–68.

Frieling, Heinrich. *Psychologische Raumgestaltung und Farbdynamik.* Göttingen: Musterschmidt Verlag, 1957.

———. "Farbgebung im OP—im Behandlungsbereich." *ZFA Zeitschrift für Allgemeinmedizin,* 52 Jahrgang, Heft 11 (20 April 1976): 582–85.

———. *Licht und Farbe am Arbeitsplatz.* Bad Wörishofen: Verlagsgemeinschaft für Wirtschaftspublizistik, 1982.

———. *Farbe am Arbeitsplatz.* Munich: Bayerisches Staatsministerium für Arbeit und Sozialordnung, 1984.

Gerard, R. "The Differential Effects of Colored Lights on Physiological Functions." Ph.D. diss., University of California at Los Angeles, 1957.

Glass, Penny, et al. "Effect of Bright Light in the Hospital Nursery on the Incidence of Retinopathy of Prematurity." *The New England Journal of Medicine,* 313 (August 1985): 401–4.

Goldstein, K. "Some Experimental Observations Concerning the Influence of Colors on the Function of the Organism." *Occupational Therapy and Rehabilitation* 21 (1942): 147–51.

Graves, Maitland. *Color Fundamentals.* New York: McGraw-Hill Book Company, Inc., 1952.

Hartmann, Erwin. *Beleuchtung am Arbeitsplatz.* Munich: Bayerisches Staatsministerium für Arbeit und Sozialordnung, 1982.

Hellman, Hal. "Guiding Light." *Psychology Today* (April 1982): 22–28.

Hodr, R. "Phototherapy of Hyperbilirubinemia in Premature Infants." *Ceskoslovenská Pediatrie* 26 (February 1971): 80–82.

Hollwich, Fritz. *The Influence of Ocular Light Perception on Metabolism in Man and in Animals.* New York: Springer Verlag, 1980.

Hollwich, Fritz, and B. Dieckhues. "The Effect of Natural and Artificial Light via the Eye on the Hormonal and Metabolic Balance of Animal and Man." *Ophthalmologica* 180 (1980): 188–97.

Hughes, Philip C. *Lighting and the Work Environment.* North Bergen, N.J.: Duro-Test Corporation, 1982.

———. "An Examination of the Beneficial Action of Natural Light on the Psychobiological System of Man." Paper accepted for presentation at Quadrennial Meeting of the Commission Internationale de l'Eclairage, Amsterdam, August 1983.

Hughes, Philip C., and Robert M. Neer. "Lighting for the Elderly: A Psychological Approach to Lighting." *Human Factors* 23 (1981): 65–85.

International Business Machines Corp. *Human Factors of Workstations with Visual Displays.* International Business Machines Corp., 1978, 1979, 1984.

Itten, Johannes. *The Art of Color.* New York: Reinhold Publishing Corp., 1961.

———. *The Elements of Color.* New York: Van Nostrand Reinhold Co., 1970.

Jacobs, K.W., and F.E. Hustmyer. "Effects of Four Psychological Primary Colors on GSR, Heart Rate and Respiration Rate." *Perceptual and Motor Skills* 38 (1974): 763–66.

Jones, Tom D. *The Art of Light and Color.* New York: Van Nostrand Reinhold Co., 1972.

Kleiber, Douglas A., et al. "Lamps—Their Effect on Social Interaction and Fatigue." *Lighting Design and Application* 4 (1974): 51–53.

Krueger, Helmut, and Wolf Müller-Limmroth. *Arbeiten mit dem Bildschirm—aber richtig!* Munich: Bayerisches Staatsministerium für Arbeit und Sozialordnung, 1983.

Küller, Rikard. "The Use of Space—Some Physiological and Philosophical Aspects." Paper presented at the Third International Architectural Psychology Conference, Université Louis Pasteur, Strasbourg, France, June 1976.

———. "Psycho-Physiological Conditions in Theatre Construction." Paper presented at the Eighth World Congress of the International Federation for Theatre Research, Munich, September 1977.

———. *Non-Visual Effects of Light and Colour.* Annotated bibliography. Document D15:81. Stockholm: Swedish Council for Building Research, 1981.

Küppers, Harald. *Color: Origin, Systems, Uses.* London: Van Nostrand Reinhold Ltd., 1973.

Lawson, D.E.M., A.A. Paul, and T.J. Cole. "Relative Contributions of Diet and Sunlight to Vitamin D State in the Elderly." *British Medical Journal* 2 (1979): 303–5.

Lewy, Alfred J., et al. "Bright Artificial Light Treatment of a Manic-Depressive Patient with a Seasonal Mood Cycle." *American Journal of Psychiatry* 139 (1982): 1496–98.

Lewy, Alfred J., et al. "Supersensitivity to Light: Possible Trait Marker for Manic-Depressive Illness." *American Journal of Psychiatry* 142 (June 1985): 725–27.

Loomis, W.F. "Rickets." *Scientific American* 223 (December 1970): 77–91.

Macaulay, Jim, and John Pliniussen. "Terminal Usage: Pro's or Con's." *Cost and Management* 8 (March/April 1984): 49–52.

Mahnke, Frank H. "Color in Medical Facilities." *Interior Design* 52 (April 1981): 256–63.

Mason, Peter. *The Light Fantastic.* Ringwood: Penguin Books Australia Ltd, 1981.

Mayron, L.W., et al. "Caries Reduction in School Children." *Applied Radiology/Nuclear Medicine* (July/August 1975).

Mayron, L.W., et al. "Light, Radiation and Academic Behavior." *Academic Therapy* 10 (Fall 1974): 33–47.

Moruzzi, G., and H.W. Magoun. "Brain Stem Reticular Formation and Activation of the EEG." *Electroencephalography and Clinical Neurophysiology* 1 (1949): 455–73.

Neer, R.M., et al. "Stimulation by Artificial Lighting of Calcium Absorption in Elderly Human Subjects." *Nature* 229 (January 1971): 255–57.

New York Committee for Occupational Safety and Health. *Health*

Protection for Operators of VDTs–CRTs. New York Committee for Occupational Safety and Health, Inc., 1980.

Ott, John N. *Health and Light: The Effects of Natural and Artificial Light on Man and Other Living Things*. New York: Pocket Books, 1976.

———. 'The Dual Function of the Eyes." *The Southern Journal of Optometry* (June 1979): 8–13.

———. *Light, Radiation, and You*. Old Greenwich, C.T.: Devin-Adair, Publishers, 1982.

———. "Color and Light: Their Effects on Plants, Animals and People." *The International Journal of Biosocial Research* 7 (1985): 1–35.

Pierman, Brian C., ed. *Color in the Health Care Environment*. NBS Special Publication 516. U.S. Department of Commerce/National Bureau of Standards, 1978.

Porter, Tom, and Byron Mikellides. *Color for Architecture*. New York: Van Nostrand Reinhold Co., 1976.

Rood, Ogden. *Modern Chromatics*. 1879. Reprint edited and annotated by Faber Birren. New York: Van Nostrand Reinhold Co., 1973.

Rosenthal, Norman E., et al. "Seasonal Affective Disorder: A Description of the Syndrome and Preliminary Findings with Light Therapy." *Archives of General Psychiatry* 41 (January 1984): 72–80.

Rosenthal, Norman E., et al. "Antidepressant Effects of Light in Seasonal Affective Disorder." *American Journal of Psychiatry* 142 (February 1985): 163–70.

Schaie, K. Warner. "Scaling the Association Between Colors and Mood-Tones." *American Journal of Psychology* 74 (1961): 266–73.

Sharon, I.M., R.P. Feller, and S.W. Burney. "The Effects of Light of Different Spectra on Caries Incidence in the Golden Hamster." *Archives Oral. Biology* (1971): 1427–32.

Sharpe, Deborah T. *The Psychology of Color and Design*. Chicago: Nelson-Hall, 1974.

Sisson, Thomas R.C. "Hazards to Vision in the Nursery." *The New England Journal of Medicine* 313 (August 1985): 444–45.

Sivik, L. "Color Connotations and Perceptive Variables." *AIC Color* 1, 2 (1969): 1064–72.

———. *Color Meaning and Perceptual Color Dimensions: A Study of Color Samples.* Göteborg Psychological Reports. Göteborg: University of Göteborg, 1974.

———. *Color Meaning and Perceptual Color Dimensions: A Study of Exterior Colors.* Göteborg Psychological Reports. Göteborg: University of Göteborg, 1974.

———. *Measuring the Meaning of Colors: Reliability and Stability.* Göteborg Psychological Reports. Göteborg: University of Göteborg, 1974.

Spivack, Mayer, and Joanna Tamer. *Light and Color: A Designer's Guide.* American Institute of Architects Service Corporation, AIA Press Division, 1984.

Thachenkary, C.S., and S.E. Harris. "Rise of Automated Office Accompanied by Continued Debate over Possible VDT Related Health Hazards." *Computerworld* 18 (November 26, 1984).

Thorington, Luke. "Light, Biology, and People, Part I." *Lighting Design and Application* 3:11 (1973):19–23.

———. "Light, Biology, and People, Part II." *Lighting Design and Application* 3:12 (1973): 31–36.

———. "Artificial Lighting—What Color and Spectrum?" *Lighting Design and Application* (November 1975).

Thorington, Luke, Louis Parascandola, and Lynn Cunningham. "The Illuminant in the Prevention and Phototherapy of Hyperbilirubinemia." *Illuminating Engineering* (April 1971): 240–50.

———. "Visual and Biologic Aspects of an Artificial Sunlight Illuminant." *Journal of the Illuminating Engineering Society* (October 1971): 33–41.

Varley, Helen, ed. *Color.* Los Angeles: Knapp Press, 1980.

Volkova, N.V. "Experience in the Use of Erythemic Ultraviolet Radiation in the General Lighting System of a Machine Shop" (translated by Duro-Test Corp.). *Gigiena i Sanitariya*, 32 (October 1967): 109–111.

Williamson, Samuel. *Light and Color in Nature and Art.* New York: John Wiley and Sons, 1983.

Wright, W.D. *The Measurement of Color.* New York: Van Nostrand Reinhold Co., 1969.

Wurtman, Richard J. "Biological Implications of Artificial Illumination." Paper presented at the National Technical Conference of the Illuminating Engineering Society, Phoenix, Arizona, September 9–12, 1968.

―――. "The Pineal and Endocrine Function." *Hospital Practice* 4 (January 1969): 32–37.

―――. "Environmental Lighting and Neuroendocrine Function: Relationship Between Spectrum of Light Source and Gonadal Growth." *Endocrinology* 86 (December 1969): 1218–21.

Wurtman, Richard J., and Robert M. Neer. "Good Light and Bad." *The New England Journal of Medicine* 282 (February 1970): 394–95.

Zamkova, M.A., and E.I. Krivitskaya. "Effect of Irradiation by Ultraviolet Erythema Lamps on the Working Ability of School Children" (translated by Duro-Test Corp.). *Gigiena i Sanitariya* 31 (April 1966): 41–44.

Zekowski, Gerry. "Lighting for CRTs—Another View." *Lighting Design and Application* (November 1981): 28–32.

Index